Worcester Moments

RIVER, RELIGION AND ROYALTY

ANDREW REEKES

To the historians of the King's School

Published by West Midlands History Limited
Minerva Mill Innovation Centre, Alcester B60 9JP, Warwickshire, UK.

ISBN: 978-1-905036-76-9

Cover image: Tomasz Janicki, Worcester based photographer. www.tomaszjanickiphoto.co.uk
Printed by: Caric Press Limited, Merthyr Tydfil, Wales.

Contents

Acknowledgements

Mike Gibbs has been a generous and enthusiastic patron of scores of authors in the West Midlands, and never more so than with this project, which he has wholeheartedly supported from its inception. History publishing in the Midlands will be immeasurably the poorer on his imminent retirement. Jenni Butterworth, my editor, has once again been a supportive, demanding and percipient critic, and the text of *Worcester Moments* has greatly benefited from her help, while Justine Pick, who has sourced the images has been ingenious and imaginative in her pursuit of the best illustrative material. I am also grateful to the librarians and archivists of the Hive in Worcester for their friendly assistance, to David Morrison, the librarian of the Worcester Cathedral Library, to David Hallmark, a fount of knowledge about the city's history, and to Colin Caldicott for sharing family archives relating to the contested General Election result of 1906. Finally, I would like to thank Matthew Armstrong, the former Headmaster of the King's School, for his infectious and oft-repeated conviction that this particular episodic interpretation of Worcester's history had real potential; his tragically early death in August 2019 is a great personal blow, as it is to the school and to the city.

Introduction

Image produced by kind permission of Tudor House Museum from its Changing Face of Worcester collection - www.cfow.org.uk

Aerial view of Worcester, its layout dominated by the Cathedral and River Severn.

The idea for such a book as this was conceived some fifty years ago when I was studying A-Level History in the shadow of Worcester Cathedral. I became aware even then of History being made around me. In the first week after joining the King's School I attended a whole school assembly in which our Headmaster fulminated on the 'desecration of historic Worcester' as planners ('vandals') conspired to tear down dozens of medieval and Tudor buildings in the shadow of the Cathedral, as part of the Council's programme of city modernisation. It made a great impact on me. A few years later it was difficult not to be conscious of the waves of protest lapping at the Watergate, after-shocks from across the river at the County Ground, where thousands loyally supported their anti-apartheid champion Basil D'Oliveira. But curriculum History somehow failed to connect the city to the great events in our national narrative. We were, it is true, inspirationally taught about the Henrician Reformation and the English Civil

War, but of Worcester's own famous Priory, and later, of the city's central part in Charles I's tragedy and the defeat of his young son in 1651, there was barely a mention. I wished I had known more back then, and I regretted not doing something to make good the deficit. So, *Worcester Moments* is aimed at anyone who wishes to understand the many ways in which Worcester and the city's people have featured prominently in the country's history.

I have rejected a continuous century-by-century narrative but have instead focused on episodes which either highlight the city's impact on our Island story or the contribution of some of her most influential progeny in the world beyond the West Midlands; taken together, these twenty moments illustrate some important themes in English history. Predictably they start at Worcester's inception, when it first became significant under Mercian kings. For the next millennium much of what was noteworthy in Worcester's story revolves around its great Cathedral foundation; only the River Severn, on whose banks the city grew up, proves an even more pervasive presence throughout its history, serving as a vital thoroughfare for trade and communication, and as a prominent geopolitical feature to be forded, defended, and fought over. It is an interesting reflection on historical continuity that in Worcester's late Roman/Anglo-Saxon times the settlement developed as a defensive site against Marcher and Viking marauders, and that more than a thousand years later – in 1939 – pill boxes and secret hides were being constructed along its waterways and roads in anticipation of the city's, and the country's, last stand against an invading German army.

Worcester Moments retells how Worcester became one of Britain's largest and most influential dioceses, dominating the West Midlands and the Marches, and how a succession of great bishops – Dunstan, Oswald and Wulstan – had a profound impact on England's spiritual life, and in the latter's case, also on her political life. *Worcester Moments* records instances of royal favour which span centuries – from Penda, Aethelred and Aethelflaeda, from William the Conqueror to King John, Henry VII, Elizabeth I and the Stuart kings, for one of whom, Charles I, Worcester was 'the 'Faithful City,' while for another, his son Charles II, it was a painful reminder of crushing military defeat. Worcester's importance extends beyond any royal connection; its sufferings in the Reformation, and then the educational renaissance prompted by the Priory's dissolution, perfectly epitomise the consequences of a disastrous policy affecting the whole nation.

Worcester citizens led the settlement of a New World across the Atlantic, were at the forefront of English church and secular music, articulated the resistance to Stuart tyranny and helped frame the charter of English liberties. They opened up the newly industrialised Black Country and Birmingham to a wider export market via water-borne communications, and developed internationally renowned porcelain, condiment, metal-working and clothing industries. Worcester men held the 'Thin Red Line' when all seemed lost on the Western Front in October 1914, and found fame for robust, manly Christian ministry in the extremity of front line trenches. The last chapter narrates the story of a man who Worcester adopted and who personified resistance to the iniquities of apartheid. The book reflects both on Worcester's emergence as a notable industrial centre for broadcloth and gloving and also as a typical small borough Conservative constituency, whose civic dignity and Imperial pride Elgar captured in his *Pomp and Circumstance Marches*, but whose unhappy history of electoral fraud and corruption became nationally notorious with the Parliamentary enquiry into the 1906 General Election result.

Although certain episodes selected themselves, the final choice of twenty historic moments was not straightforward. I had assumed that I would write about the Three Choirs Festival, the world's oldest continuous music festival, now nearly 300 years old, but the more I read, the more I realised that it would be both wrong and impractical to shear Worcester off from a story in which the three cathedrals are inextricably inter-woven. Despite the towering figure of Edward Elgar, Worcester's contribution to the Festival was no more remarkable than, for example, the Gloucester of Howells, Parry and Vaughan Williams and it would be unhistoric to pretend otherwise.

From the outset I had planned to devote a chapter to the Cathedral itself, but although I still regret I have not found space for 'the Thirteenth-century Tremulous Hand', a famous scribe in the Cathedral's scriptorium, or indeed for a paragraph or two on its renowned Cathedral Library, I came to the conclusion that so many of the early chapters drew on the Cathedral's history that a chapter solely dedicated to it would involve tedious duplication. Lastly, I had thought I would write about the political pollsters' construct of 'Worcester woman', a supposedly typical woman voter in the C2 socio-economic category who was thought to favour the policies of Tony Blair in the era of New Labour ascendancy. Having defined her, and having recorded that this imaginary demographic typifier was thought to exist in large numbers in Worcester, I found there was little more to say. Certainly, not enough to merit a chapter.

The moments which appear here comprise a tale stretching across 1,400 years, during which time Worcester – by dint of its strategic position and its diocesan leadership – has assumed a prominent position in the West Midlands. It might justifiably be argued that it has 'punched above its weight', for its contribution to our Island story appears uncommonly significant for a city with a population of only 100,000 souls.

Early Worcester

Image produced by kind permission of Tudor House Museum from its Changing Face of Worcester collection – www.cfow.org.uk

The 14th-century Edgar Tower, entrance to the Cathedral precincts.

From its small beginnings in Roman times, Worcester grew into a wealthy trading and industrial settlement – among the twenty largest towns of early Tudor England. Its medieval development is explained by two important factors: its location and the influence of the Church.

Worcester was fortunate to be at the centre of a communications network. The River Severn allowed access to, and trade with, Bewdley in the Midlands upstream and Bristol downstream. Equally, the settlement flourished as a Severn bridging point, to Herefordshire and to South Wales as well as a route up the River Teme, via Ludlow into Central Wales. The bridge at Worcester was therefore used by many routes from Wales to London and to the Midlands and the North, and Worcester was a hub for a road system serving Bristol, London, Hereford, Ludlow, Shrewsbury, Lichfield and Coventry.

This was significant economically and politically. Worcester developed as a market for agricultural products from the surrounding counties, and for the goods made by craftsmen in the town and neighbouring villages. The thriving fairs in the town were recognised by King Richard I in 1189 when he granted Worcester a royal charter, and by Henry III in 1227 in another charter which created the town's first merchant guild. Population grew as immigrants from the surrounding countryside were attracted to settle in a prosperous urban environment. One further indication of Worcester's prosperity is the size of its Jewish community in the thirteenth century, which was the target of an infamous massacre by Simon de Montfort's sons and followers in 1264. By the early sixteenth century Worcester had emerged as one of the country's foremost broadcloth production centres, with a larger percentage of its citizens engaged in the industry (around 50%) than in any other English town. The industry's success was largely due to supplies of the highest-quality wool in England, brought downriver from Shrewsbury and Bridgnorth and across the bridge from Herefordshire.

Worcester's enviable position astride the Severn, close to the borders between England and Wales, would have political ramifications too. At various times in its first millennium its distance from London, and also from Viking marauding, would be an asset; so too would be the fact that it was a useful forward base from which to deal both with rebellion in Wales and with over-ambitious Marcher Lords. Several of the Medieval Worcester moments which follow illustrate this: for Aethelred and Aethelflaeda their burh at Worcester would be a defensible base from which to project a counter-attack against the Danes in the North Midlands; for Norman conquerors, a castle keep high on the eastern bank of the Severn at Worcester was a necessity to secure these border lands; for King John Worcester was a safe haven when much of Eastern England was controlled by rebel barons; while for Henry III facing the Welsh national revival under Llewellyn the Great from 1215, and later for his son Edward I in countering Llewellyn ap Gruffydd in 1277, Worcester was the natural base for a military headquarters. That Prince Arthur, son and heir of Henry VII, exercised power in Ludlow – just to the north of Worcester – and was then buried in the city, illustrates the importance a king, bent on pacifying his lands after the Wars of the Roses, attached to an active, visible royal presence in a turbulent, unreliable part of his kingdom.

Geography alone does not explain Worcester's increasing significance in these centuries. Archbishop Theodore's decision to make Worcester the centre of a new diocese to minister to the West Midlands in 680 probably reflected the existing importance of the settlement as a local capital. Across the Anglo-Saxon and Norman periods successive cathedral churches gave physical expression to that hegemony and the impressive scale of the building explains why several kings used it as a stage for theatrical moments of state-craft. For example, Henry II revived the old ceremonial crown-wearing of the English kings in the Cathedral in 1158 to reinforce a long tradition underpinning his royal authority, and to consolidate his supremacy over restless barons. John chose to be buried there in full pomp and solemnity while his son, Henry III, resolved differences with Llewellyn the Great in the Cathedral in 1218; Edward I received Welsh submission in the nave and the Yorkists solemnised their incipient rebellion there. Ludlow was deemed an insufficiently grand final resting place for a Tudor prince and Arthur was instead interred with great ceremony in Worcester's Cathedral, his tomb acting as an expression of propaganda for Henry VII's pacification project.

Worcester also played a significant part in the national revival of monastic discipline and – by extension – of scholarship and learning in an England newly united by Alfred the Great. From the time of Archbishops Dunstan and Oswald in the tenth century, Worcester's priory, and its library and scriptorium, became a leading centre of culture and of study and Oswald appears to have been the original inspiration for Worcester's enduring reputation for music. These bishops, and a number of successors in the next five centuries, became valued advisors to the king at court; one bishop of Worcester, Giulio Medici, even became Pope, as Clement VII, in the early sixteenth century.

The Church's direct contribution to the growth of the settlement at Worcester was economic. Across the Middle Ages, as it accumulated grants of manors and other gifts, the Priory became one of the largest landowners in the West of England. Certainly, by Bishop Oswald's time in the tenth century, the needs of the Priory and its retainers for provisions and other necessaries had stimulated the growth of a market which drew upon the farming and trades of the surrounding counties; the Priory also seems to have encouraged the building of housing to the north of the priory church. Visitors and pilgrims to the Cathedral greatly promoted economic activity in the town, especially with the evolution of the cults of SS Oswald and Wulstan in the eleventh and twelfth centuries, and with the exploitation in the late Middle Ages of the Cathedral's shrine to the Virgin Mary. Nor was it just the Cathedral and Priory which made of Worcester a prominent religious centre; its parish churches and the houses of the Grey and Black Friars, as well as the monastic hospitals, had a role too.

Worcester's Emergence

The picture we have of Worcester's origins is drawn from a multitude of different sources – written, archaeological and place-name evidence. The early centuries of its existence encompass a history of iron-age tribes, the Roman conquest in the first century, and then the arrival of Anglo-Saxon settlers in the late-fifth and sixth centuries. Once the Romans had withdrawn at the start of the fifth century, place-name evidence and surviving artefacts attest that the West Midlands became a fusion of surviving British with Germanic newcomers. Worcester, *civitate Wegornensi*, was but a small western settlement; it was soon a part of a new Anglo-Saxon kingdom, that of Mercia, centred on Tamworth, Lichfield and Repton.

It seems that Worcester's origins lie with the Dobunni, an iron-age tribal group, before a minor Roman settlement was founded there; it would appear that this old tribal unit outlived the Romans, to survive into the era of the Hwicce. Early Worcester was a very small town on the banks of the Severn with a market function and a well-developed iron industry. There may have been a bridge over the Severn at this time, though later Anglo-Saxon charters, in recording a *gelad* (crossing-point), may have only been referring to a ferry. Equally unclear is whether Worcester was a centre of the British church during the Roman occupation. But in the century after their withdrawal, Worcester does appear to have become an early ecclesiastical and administrative centre for the British community. Two probable Christian burials excavated beneath Worcester's current Cathedral suggest late 5th or early 6th century dating. And while there is precious little evidence of any kind for these transition years from Roman to Anglo-Saxon occupation, there are some clues in the foregoing narrative as to why Worcester would emerge as a significant regional centre under the new Germanic dispensation from the end of the 6th century onwards.

Gildas, the British monk, described the impact of these Anglo-Saxon invaders as he saw them:

> 'a fire heaped up and nurtured by the hand of impious easterners spread from sea to sea. It devastated town and country around about and, once it was alight it did not die down until it burned almost the whole surface of the island and was licking the western ocean with its fierce red tongue'.

However, there seems reason to doubt whether the arrival of these incomers throughout the sixth century was one of violent conquest in the West Midlands;

instead there appears to have been a gradual accommodation of the two peoples, British and Germanic, and over time 'Germanic cultural traits were gradually assimilated,' as John Hunt has recently written in his history of Mercia. The mix of native British and incoming Anglo-Saxons who settled in the West Midlands gave rise to the people of the Hwicce who were – it seems – welded into a coherent unit by Penda, the formidable pagan King of the Mercians around 628, as an English buffer against the Welsh. Despite his lack of personal Christian conviction he was prepared to tolerate the surviving British church organisation and to permit the Hwicce to develop their own cultural identity. For well over a century the rulers of the Hwicce claimed to be kings but, by 805, documents suggest that the Hwicce were ruled by ealdormen subject to the overlordship of the kings of Mercia.

For our purposes, Worcester had by the end of the 7th century developed as the most important urban centre for the Hwicce, whose lands comprised Worcestershire bounded to the west by the Malverns and the Abberley Hills to the north, by Gloucestershire (except the Forest of Dean) to the south, and south Warwickshire to Worcester's east. There were rival claims to leadership in the West Midlands; Gloucester (which was probably too close to the West Saxons) or Winchcombe (a favourite of the Mercian kings), but Worcester's pre-eminence was greatly assisted by the foundation of an episcopal see by Archbishop Theodore in 680. It was part of his reorganisation of the English church. The medieval diocesan boundaries he defined then appear to have preserved those of the kingdom of the Hwicce, and their extent made Worcester an important ecclesiastical power in the region. In fact, the Hwicce seem already to have adopted the Christianity of the local British they encountered in the area, long before Theodore's diocesan reform. In his *Historia Ecclesiastica* (731), the Venerable Bede records an important meeting in 603 of representatives of the Roman and the British churches at St Augustine's Oak, on the borders of the Hwicce and the West Saxons, presumed to be Wychwood (Hwicca's wood) in Oxfordshire. At this meeting the Hwicce were employed as intermediaries. So, it seems that Theodore was establishing a new diocese in an area he knew to have a church organisation already. But he chose Worcester for other reasons too: it was close to the western frontier of Saxon England, and to the Magonsaetan, the tribe who held Herefordshire. When Theodore created Worcester's diocese he also founded the bishopric of Hereford and he clearly anticipated that the two centres would minister to much of the West of England together. In addition to all this, Worcester had some urban development already, greater than – for example – Winchcombe, and its

Photograph by Mr. Christopher Guy, Worcester Cathedral Archaeologist. Reproduced by permission of the Chapter of Worcester Cathedral (U.K.)

Aethelred and Aethelflaeda, commemorated in stained glass in the Cathedral.

Image produced by kind permission of Tudor House Museum from its Changing Face of Worcester collection- www.cfow.org.uk

18th-century view of Worcester showing two of its key medieval features, the Cathedral and the Norman castle motte.

increasing importance as an economic focus made it sensible to centre Theodore's ecclesiastical organisation there.

Theodore's reforms could not have been achieved without the support of Mercian kings. In fact, late Mercian charters record Aethelred, Penda's son, endowing a new religious house at Worcester, whose hegemony as a religious centre was quickly consolidated. In short order bishops of Worcester had assumed a prominent position, signing themselves *Episcopus Huicciorum*. By the middle of the 8th century an episcopal lease claimed Worcester to be *Metropolim Huicciorum* (capital of the Hwicce) while to the end of the century (789) the last recorded king of the Hwicce, Ealdred, was describing himself as under-king of Worcester. By then the Hwicce had been subsumed in the larger Mercian entity even though aspects of their culture and language persisted.

Worcester's growth went hand in hand with the increasing wealth of its church, which became one of the great landholders in the whole of the West Midlands, with estates across the Severn to the west, in the Vale of

Evesham, and into Warwickshire. Being the centre of the diocese led to the building of other churches in the town; certainly, five are known to have existed by the time of the Norman Conquest, consolidating Worcester's reputation as a great ecclesiastical focal point. In the 8th and 9th centuries a commercial settlement grew up to serve the Christian community and Worcester started to become a thriving market town. Topographical evidence from charter boundary clauses – painstakingly analysed by Della Hooke – shows Worcester as a hub with numerous routeways radiating in all directions: across the river into Herefordshire and Wales, along the 'red way' from the Avon valley to the South East, and from the North East via *bradan straet* to Droitwich, whose springs were numbered among the marvels of Britain in the 9th century, as were the 'wells of salt' which for centuries had been traded right across southern Britain. Those routeways facilitated Worcester's mercantile expansion, as did the development of river trade and a port at Worcester from the 8th century onwards.

Paradoxically, the Danish invasions which swept across eastern and central England in the 9th century augmented Worcester's importance. The area would prove a secure and relatively untroubled base from which Aethelred, Earl of the Mercians, and his wife Aethelflaeda, could launch counter-attacks against the Viking raiders. They did so on behalf of Alfred, the West Saxon ruler who became king of England by fighting the Danes and then ensuring peace through negotiation with Guthrum their leader. Alfred's campaign had safeguarded western Mercia and he married his daughter Aethelflaeda to the Mercian earl, so sealing an important strategic alliance which would, he hoped, keep the West Midlands firmly under his aegis. It seems that it was Alfred who won the assent of the Mercian *witan* and ordered the building of a *burh* at Worcester 'for the protection of all people'. It was fortified at some date between 884 and 899. As a consequence, Bishop Werfrith negotiated with Aethelred and Aethelflaeda that the church of St Peter's would – in return for the dedication of psalms (three times a day) and masses (every Saturday) in perpetuity – share with them 'land-rent, the fine for fighting or theft, or dishonest trading…exactly as it has been laid down as regards the market-place and streets'. They would, for their part, fortify Worcester.

The charter of 884 which stipulates these terms is of great historic importance. It is one of the earliest records of the existence of a borough court in England, spelling out the infractions with which it would have to deal; it also confirms the existence of a market at Worcester; and it sets out the duties of the townsmen as regards the maintenance of the *burh*'s walls. Although these walls and the accompanying earthen rampart on its circular course round the settlement are no long visible, there is strong archaeological evidence for this ninth-century *burh*. The charter goes on to talk of a bishop's quarter within the *burh*, and of the streets where the jurisdiction fell to the king.

A second charter of 904 is almost as significant in that among other things it describes the dimensions of plots of land given to tenants who wish to engage in trade. These plots within Worcester's north wall were unusually referred to as *haga*, a term normally applied in the West Midlands to hedges and enclosures in thickly wooded land. The similarity is in the fact that these *hagan* were fenced. Only Warwick, also a newly-constructed *burh* at this time, had such urban *hagan*. Many of these borough properties were linked to rural manors in the surrounding countryside, so that the Worcester *hagan* could well have been secure and defensible accommodation for inhabitants of the county if trouble threatened, while the country estates provided essential foodstuffs for the towns. This linkage of town and country properties will be replicated by Bishop Oswald (see next chapter) later in the century.

In that year Bishop Werfirth granted a lease of land on the river frontage (perhaps below the current Cathedral, running down the east side of the Severn to the present Diglis basin) to Aethelred and Aethelflaeda, and for the lifetime of their daughter Aelfwynn; this was to be a source of valuable profits and is another indication of Worcester's flourishing commercial life. This grant also establishes the extent to which the bishop was the greatest figure in the borough, illustrating his wealth and influence, but it and that charter of 884 record the way that – on grounds of security in dangerous times – episcopal power was now being shared with earthly lords. The lease of river frontage allowed the Mercian earls to control Worcester; they used it as a base from which to attack territories in Danelaw in the Midlands and the North, on one occasion liberating the remains of the Northumbrian saint, Oswald, from Bardney in Lincolnshire – which was controlled by the Danes – and bringing them back to the West Midlands to re-inter them in the new minster at Gloucester.

Aethelred played a major role in turning back the Viking tide in the Midlands, and his death in 911 served only to empower his extraordinary wife Aethelflaeda, who subsequently ruled as Lady of the Mercians to her death in 918. The historian Ian Walker has described this as 'one of the most unique events in medieval history'. In these years she gave material support to her brother, King Edward, who had succeeded their father Alfred the Great. She was, according to William of Malmesbury, 'a powerful accession to Edward's party, the dread of his enemies, a woman of an enlarged soul'. They shared a campaign to take the fight to the Danes, and to secure territory by creating a network of new *burhs* in an arc to the north and east of Worcester. So, she built defences at Bridgnorth, Tamworth, Stafford, Warwick, Runcorn and Chirbury, and sent an army to capture Derby in 917, which would constitute her greatest triumph.

Even if Mercia (very unlike Wessex) had a tradition of according its queens a degree of political importance, witnessing charters for example and making grants in their own names, Aethelflaeda's achievements still stand out as being exceptional. Her guardianship of Mercia freed her brother to initiate the counter-attacks against the Danes which made his reputation. It is clear that she alone ensured Mercia's independence, for Edward drew on her undoubted strength and strategic intuition; on her death he took personal control of Mercia and swept his niece Aelfwynn off to live at his court in Winchester. Although it is true that Aethelflaeda had a special affection for Gloucester, where she was buried in the Minster church of St Oswald she had founded, it is nevertheless legitimate for Worcester to lay some claim to this remarkable Mercian queen, who fortified it and used it as a military base from which to drive back the Viking interlopers.

By the mid-10th century, on the eve of Bishop Oswald's long tenure, Worcester was the established capital of a West Midland region circumscribed by Hwiccian boundaries. Its church was one of the most significant landowners in the west, its *burh* was a market centre and port, while its defences made it a natural focus of regional resistance to further foreign encroachment. There is also evidence that Worcester became a minting centre in the 10th century; by the reign of Edward the Confessor there were seven moneyers recorded at work in Worcester.

In 1041 one well-documented incident illustrates Worcester's standing on the eve of the Conquest. It became a centre of English resistance to King Harthacnut's heavy taxes. When Thurstane and Feader, two of his housecarls, arrived to collect the Danegeld in Worcester 'the multitude rose against them,' according to Valentine Green, Worcester's 18th-century historian. They fled to the Edgar Tower but were intercepted and slain and it is said that their skins were nailed to the cathedral door. The king sent a large force under Godwin and Siward, 'executioners of his vengeance,' to punish Worcester's inhabitants, but they abandoned the town and fortified themselves on Bevere Island in the Severn, two miles north of the centre. Worcester 'was rifled by the king's forces, and the streets set ablaze'. They then besieged the island; after 'warm resistance', Harthacnut's men conceded an honourable capitulation and the citizens returned to rebuild their ravaged town.

As we will now see, the leadership of two late Anglo-Saxon bishops of Worcester, Oswald and Wulstan, consolidated Worcester's regional pre-eminence, a process which had taken some five centuries of steady growth and development.

CHAPTER 2

St Oswald of Worcester

Three bishops of Worcester were weighty national figures in late Anglo-Saxon England. Dunstan, Oswald and Wulstan were all later canonised for their personal piety and for their impact on the survival and revival of the English church after the traumas of ninth-century Viking invasions.

Dunstan (909-988), abbot of Glastonbury, artist, scholar, musician and metal-worker, for centuries the English church's favourite saint, was the inspiration for the revitalisation of monastic life in England. Influenced by a stay at the newly reformed monastery at Ghent, he set about the renewal of Glastonbury from 944, establishing rigorous Benedictine discipline there before being translated to Worcester. However, his time as bishop in the West Midlands was short, before promotion to the archbishopric of Canterbury; it was not long enough to make a distinctive impact, though perhaps the most important thing Dunstan did for Worcester was to advise King Edgar in 961 to appoint Oswald as his successor. This chapter will focus on Oswald and his much lengthier tenure of the Worcester diocese, while the next chapter describes the achievement of the eleventh-century St Wulstan.

In contrast to the narratives later on in this book for which source material is plentiful, Oswald's story suffers from the imperfect nature of contemporary evidence; much has to be deduced, filled in or guessed at. Viking destruction and looting of monastic libraries especially in the North, North Midlands and the East has severely compromised the historical record of these years. In Oswald's case historians are reliant on a surviving monastic biography, that of Byrhtferth's *Vita Oswaldi*, written not in Worcester but in the abbey at Ramsey. This, and extant charter evidence, is sufficient to animate the bare bones of the saint's life, but it is not enough to provide us with an accurate date of birth (thought to be around 925).

At the very outset his background was notable. The *Liber Benefactorum*, the chronicle of Ramsey, records that his parents were Danish. Certainly, his influential uncle, Oda, Archbishop of Canterbury (941 – 958) was the son of a Viking. Nor was Oda the only senior cleric in the family; another relative had been Archbishop of York. So, Oswald was well-connected and wealthy, and Oda was from the start a powerful influence, both in instructing Oswald through 'the sacred letters from his uncle', and in directing him to a small monastery in Winchester where he was educated. It was Oda who then sent Oswald

St Oswald, depicted in a later 13th-century manuscript.

from Winchester to retrace his own youthful journey by joining the recently revived community at Fleury in the Loire. Fleury was famous both for its great library and for harbouring the remains of St Benedict, but it suffered a decline which was only reversed by Odo of Cluny in the 930s. He did so to such effect that it thereafter became a model of Benedictine excellence. Byrhtferth notes in his *Vita* that Oswald at Fleury was subject to full monastic discipline and to all personal austerities, and also that he set out to memorise the texts and settings of the liturgy practised there in order to teach them at home. The standards he learnt, and the liturgy he practised were to be the basis for the monastic reforms Oswald would introduce at Worcester, Westbury-on-Trym, six other Mercian houses, and Ramsey; they would mark him out – with Dunstan and Aethelwold of Winchester - as a key figure in the revival of monasticism in England.

Oswald would retain the love of music that Fleury awakened in him for the rest of his life; he sang beautifully himself, according to his biographer, showed an abiding interest in the singing voice, and it has been recently argued that he first established Worcester's long musical tradition. Similarly, the contact he made with Fleury continued long after Oswald returned to England, and well exemplifies the close reciprocal links the Anglo-Saxons enjoyed with the Continent, in Worcester's case involving French monastic visitors such as Abbo of Fleury while English scholars like Germanus, keen to study in the reformed Benedictine houses, passed the other way across the Channel.

Byrhtferth tells us that Oswald was summoned home in 958 by Oda, who evidently knew he was dying; Oswald learnt of Oda's death on his return, but the loss of one patron was made good by his attachment to Oscytel (also a relative), the new Archbishop of York. The chronicler went on to claim that Oswald accompanied Oscytel to Rome on his mission to obtain the pallium, the vestment bestowed by the Pope on primates as a symbol of delegated authority. There remains much doubt about whether this journey ever took place. What is sure is that Oscytel pointed Oswald on another sort of journey entirely, for by introducing him to Dunstan – on whom Oswald made a favourable impression – he opened up the possibility that, when Dunstan was promoted from Worcester to Canterbury in 961, he would recommend that King Edgar engage Oswald as his successor.

Historians consider Oswald's 31-year tenure at Worcester (961-992) to be significant on a number of counts. One particular interest was the creation of the Oswaldslow, and the leading authority on this, Patrick Wormald, has written that the 'bishop of Worcester's triple hundred of Oswaldslow constitutes some of the most blood-soaked acres in English medieval historiography'. For many years, historians had been deceived by an Anglo-Saxon forgery, which found its way into the *Domesday Book* account of Oswaldslow. The implication was that the triple hundred was a unique administrative unit in Anglo-Saxon England, where the king had ceded to the bishop all rights of jurisdiction. Only in recent years was that forgery exposed.

The facts are that Oswald, early on in his tenure as bishop, started granting leases to family members to establish a close-knit network of individuals throughout the three counties centred on Worcester. They held their leases for a term of three lives, while agreeing in return that they 'will be humbly subject to the commands of the bishop, for the fulfilment of the service due to him or the king'. The bishop took the profits of justice in Oswaldslow, and won the right to command the *fyrd*, the hundred's troops in time of war; by so doing he was building for himself and the king a loyal tenancy who would help resist not only ambitious nobles like Aelfhere, who (according to the Anglo-Saxon Chronicle) 'broke God's law, hindered monastic life, destroyed monasteries and dispersed West Mercian monks,' and the future depredations of Viking raiders. Now we may conclude that although Oswaldslow was not a unique judicial immunity, beyond the reach of the king and his sheriff, nevertheless Oswald was effectively an important regional viceroy for King Edgar; the latter much preferred to use bishops for the role because unlike nobles, there were no children to inherit their local power bases.

It is likely that his appointment in 972 to the archbishopric of York – to be held in addition to the episcopacy of Worcester – was also one of political calculation on King Edgar's part. York was impoverished by struggles with Viking invaders; Worcester's income would shore up depleted finances. More than this, the allegiance of the North was questionable. It was important to have a proven loyalist like Oswald to represent royalist interests. Byrhtferth reinforces the impression that Edgar especially trusted Oswald as a diplomatic ambassador when he writes that the King sent the bishop to the German Emperor in 972 to agree a *pactum pacis*, perhaps prior to Oswald's journey to Rome both to receive the pallium as Archbishop of York and to arrange the long-awaited coronation of Edgar as king, at Bath. The location of that coronation well exemplifies the peripatetic nature of kingship in these turbulent years.

Oswald was not simply an important political figure. Ecclesiastical historians see him at the forefront of the monastic revival, helping King Edgar in his policy of countering the growing secularism which had infected the tenth-century English church. Dunstan had little time to reform Worcester, but Oswald had decades to bring about renewal, which involved gradually replacing the incumbent married clerks with monks; at Worcester unlike in Winchester, there was no 'big bang' bringing about a 'mass redundancy' of clergy, but a process of replacement over perhaps thirty years. It seems that Oswald created a new cathedral precinct in the city when he started the building of a larger edifice, St Mary's, alongside the old cathedral church of St Peter's. In this sharply defined precinct there was a fresh emphasis on prayer, burial, sanctuary; and here Oswald introduced a young generation of monks, who would be subject to the revised monastic discipline drafted by Aethelwold and sanctioned by the Council of Winchester: the *Regularis Concordia* of 973, in the composition of which Oswald played a small part. He ensured these monks were exposed to a stimulating education by importing preachers, mathematicians and even astronomers from Fleury, while – as we have seen – he did much to establish a choral tradition among the monks of his cathedral church of St Mary.

They came from one of his own foundations, Ramsey Abbey, in Cambridgeshire. Oswald had a major role in reviving religious activity in East Anglia where many religious houses had suffered cruelly at the hands of the Danes. He chose the site carefully; a peninsula in fen waterlands, it had fertile soil and a plenitude of fish and fowl, it was intensely quiet to encourage contemplation, and he loved it so much that he served for a time as its abbot, whilst retaining his other responsibilities. He was equally important in revivifying the failing monastic house at Westbury-on-Trym (near Bristol), persuading Germanus, an English monk originally from Winchester, whom he had met at Fleury, to take up the challenge at Westbury. Both foundations flourished, with Ramsey becoming a notably rich and successful monastery. In addition, he introduced Benedictine reforms to Winchcombe, Gloucester, Deerhurst, Pershore and Evesham.

Oswald gave an example of holiness to the Benedictines who followed him. At Worcester he earned a reputation for encouraging lay communion, the participation of lay people in the sacrament, and in the washing of the feet of the poor; it is recorded that he died in Lent while engaged in doing just that. He was also famed as a preacher. Byrhtferth records that he preached in the cathedral cemetery because the existing church was too small, which explains Oswald's decision to build St Mary's, as well as suggesting that the city of Worcester itself now accommodated a sizeable population. His chronicler documented Oswald's joy at completing the new building by 983: 'Our Lord and our Redeemer has granted so great a boon of his loving kindness and I have been able to bring to completion the basilica in honour of Mary which I have established in my episcopal see, namely in the monastery in Worcester. The holiness exemplified above sufficiently impressed monks at Worcester that in his last years an expectation grew up there that he would be raised to a sainthood. We are told that on his death in 992 such was the grief in the city that traders, workers, women weavers stopped work and wept, and a white dove hovered over the funeral procession. A new Worcester bishop from Peterborough, Ealdwulf, seems vigorously to have promulgated the cult of Oswald around the end of the tenth century, translating his remains to a new mausoleum in 1002. A successful cult attracting pilgrims was a useful money-spinner; this one remained localised in Mercia, especially in and around Worcester, although it had its adherents in Ramsey, York and Fleury.

Oswald more than any other tenth-century bishop had a profound impact on the development of the city of Worcester. He used the city to the north of the cathedral precincts to house and reward his retainers; in addition, monks from the cathedral priory held houses, to which were attached rural landholdings. The expectation was that this land would provide the means by which to sustain Oswald's tenants. So, produce from the estates would be brought into Worcester for consumption; in their turn rural producers were able to purchase goods in Worcester. Here was the stimulus to the *burh*'s growth as a market-place, and indications of the city's expansion in Oswald's time can be found through the results of archaeological research in Sidbury in the south-east and Mealcheapen in the north-east of Worcester.

Oswald helped establish the cathedral priory at Worcester as one of the leading religious houses in the land. Beyond the West Midlands he was a significant figure in the reform of the Anglo-Saxon church. For centuries his shrine at Worcester drew pilgrims and was the scene of miracles. However, in the sixteenth century Reformation saint-worship, the veneration of relics, and the notion of pilgrimage to shrines, proved anathema to Protestants and Oswald and Wulstan's remains suffered iconoclastic destruction, along with their reputations.

CHAPTER 3

Wulstan – Last of the Anglo-Saxons

In June 1218, long after Wulstan's death, Worcester's newly renovated cathedral was re-consecrated in the presence of a king, young Henry III, and of an impressive company of bishops and abbots. Wulstan's body was translated to a shrine near the high altar, as befitted a recently canonised saint. The scale of the ceremony and the importance of the guests who attended tell us much about Wulstan's reputation: he had been the favourite saint of Henry's father King John (see later chapter) and by the start of the thirteenth century Worcester was second only to Canterbury as a centre for pilgrimage.

Yet Wulstan was more than a saint around whom stories of miraculous healing multiplied. He was equally important as a church leader with national authority, and as a political figure. For his long tenure of the see at Worcester coincided with the Norman Conquest. Wulstan demonstrated a suppleness and resilience which ensured that, while the overwhelming majority of leading Anglo-Saxons – bishops as well as nobles – were swiftly replaced by the conquering class, he survived and prospered, to become every bit as valuable an advisor to William I as he had been to Harold before him. By the time he died in 1095 he was, in the words of a contemporary, Eadmer of Canterbury, 'the one sole survivor of the Old Fathers of the English people'. In his person he came to represent continuity, transmitting the traditions and values of the Anglo-Saxon church of Bede and Cuthbert to the new Norman order where they were absorbed and venerated.

We know about Worcester's most famous saint from the *Life of St Wulstan*, written by the leading historian of his age, William of Malmesbury (1095-1143), who himself relied on the testimony of a monk, Coleman. William says that Coleman 'deserves the fullest credence, for as a disciple he knew his master's ways closely and as his chaplain for fifteen years he knew his religion'. Coleman's *Life* is now lost; however, through William's transcription, we learn that Wulstan was born in Itchington, Warwickshire in 1008. His mother may well have been sister of another Wulstan, the Archbishop of York, an influential advisor to Ethelred. The young Wulstan first learnt his letters at Evesham, and then 'his tender mind was trained in a more perfect learning' in the monastery at Peterborough, before coming to Worcester. William of Malmesbury recounts Wulstan's life-story through a sequence of episodes designed to illuminate Wulstan's emerging saintliness, for his *Life* follows the tropes of conventional hagiography.

Much is made of Wulstan's moral purity and his battle to resist temptation. William relates a lengthy tale of how the youthful Wulstan resisted the 'beckoning eyes and wanton gestures of a damsel of the neighbourhood intent on making a shipwreck of his modesty, tempting him with sinful pleasures'. Clerical celibacy would remain an important issue for Wulstan; he insisted on it in his diocese, and the fact that the new Norman Archbishop Lanfranc prioritised it was a strong recommendation.

After he had become a priest through the good offices of the Bishop of Worcester, his patron Brihtheah, he was intent on taking the monk's habit. Brihtheah, we are told, 'came to love him for his graces of the soul,' and tried to dissuade him from following his parents into a monastery, instead offering him a rich benefice in the diocese. Wulstan prevailed and, once a monk at Worcester, his abilities and his godliness marked him out. He became first the monastery's schoolmaster, then the precentor and the sacrist, indications both of his scholarship and some musical inclination. Just as important were signs of rigorous self-discipline and devotion. 'He passed his days fasting and whole nights watching.' It is possible that mortification of the flesh and sleep-deprivation explain his surreal battle with the Devil himself who, it is related, came to him in the cathedral church: 'the enemy fell upon him, winding his sinewy arms about the saint's body, wasted with fasting. At last the grisly shadow gave way before Wulstan's valiant faith.' But the Devil apparently trampled on Wulstan's foot, poison entering his very bones, and a sore developing thereafter.

Brihtheah went on to appoint Wulstan head of the Priory at Worcester, where 'he reformed many things that were amiss both within the [religious] house and without'. Moral laxity was firmly dealt with, whilst he personally gave an example to the monks of pastoral care and evangelical mission. 'He would often prolong his day in the cathedral church, till noon, even to evensong, if he could help those who had suffered violence, or to baptise the children of the poor'. He also became a notable preacher; he felt that the people were falling away from the church for lack of regular preaching and so, on Sundays and all the great festivals, 'he poured into their ears the counsels of salvation,' (whilst also) 'thundering against sinners and sprinkling refreshing rain on the elect'. It was from his time as prior that stories began to be told of his healing powers.

He vigorously restored the monastery's finances, damaged by the taxation imposed by the Danish king Cnut in the years before the Norman Conquest, and repaired and extended the buildings, as we will see. We

Oswald and Wulstan, Worcester's two important saints, depicted in stained glass in the Cathedral.

also know that – following on from the monastic revival at Worcester initiated by Oswald – he increased the number of monks from twelve to almost fifty across his long association with the Priory.

In 1062 Wulstan was consecrated as Bishop of Worcester by his predecessor, Ealdred, who was also Archbishop of York. Wulstan had greatly impressed a delegation of cardinals who had visited Ealdred at Worcester, and they recommended he appoint Wulstan to succeed him. He would remain bishop, through all subsequent political vicissitudes, for thirty-three years. That long tenure consolidated his reputation for saintliness, for William – paraphrasing Coleman – enlarges on his many holy attributes: he frequently 'drove off disease,' be it leprosy, distemper, blindness or 'idiocy'. Whenever he went around his diocese he preached a sermon or conducted a mass and signed with a cross all children brought to him, however many there were; it was said that he confirmed between 2000 and 3000 people in a day. He 'eschewed pride', refusing to wear the ermine common to his class, but contenting himself with lamb-skin, with all its appropriate connotations of the Good Shepherd. He attended two masses a day, sometimes singing a third. 'To church he would go, snow or rain, storm or tempest, whatever the state of the roads.' At the same time, he expected high standards from others, being something of a strict disciplinarian.

Other contemporary testimony confirms that William's overly reverential portrait nevertheless communicates a substantial truth, for Wulstan evidently impressed his peers by his simplicity, his humility, his guilelessness and his purity of heart. William concludes without undue exaggeration saying that 'the fame of his holiness had by his death gone throughout the land, even to the ends of the world for the Pope, the Archbishop of Bari and the Patriarch of Jerusalem sought his advocacy'.

Beyond his personal ministry he did much important work as a church leader. As prior he recovered for the monastery those lands which his predecessors had sold or given away, gathering in all charters and correspondence relating to manors which had at one time been part of the estate. He evidently had a gift for administration; when bishop, he developed a household organisation in which Coleman, his biographer, was the chancellor and Ailric, the archdeacon. Close and regular visitation of every part of the diocese ensued. Wulstan also administered law in the shire-moot. But his influence extended beyond his diocese; nationally he came to be regarded as a patriarchal figure and was called upon to perform dedications of new parish churches across the country.

He had political wiles too, which were exemplified when he saw off an attempt by the Archbishop of Canterbury, Lanfranc, to replace him as Bishop of Worcester. Legend related that Lanfranc asked Wulstan to surrender the diocese in favour of a Norman in 1075, while they were standing by Edward the Confessor's tomb in Westminster Abbey. Wulstan humbly laid his crozier on the tomb but Gundulf, ordered by Lanfranc to pick it up, was unable to lift it clear, for it was stuck fast. Lanfranc and William I then became convinced of divine approbation for Wulstan's episcopacy. Thus, he retained Worcester; he then prevailed on the King to restore to Worcester the villages lost to 'the insolence of the Danes,' and to the appropriations of his predecessor Ealdred, who had augmented the estates of the diocese of York at Worcester's expense when he had held both dioceses simultaneously. Furthermore, Wulstan persuaded Lanfranc to transfer Worcester from the archdiocese of York to Canterbury.

Wulstan had also been highly regarded by King Harold who, we are told, 'loved him above all men,' and 'would turn aside thirty miles on a journey that in converse with Wulstan he might forget the burden of his cares'. Indeed, in that fraught year of 1066 Harold called Wulstan to him 'for the fame of his holiness had found its way to the remotest tribes and he believed (Wulstan) could quell the most stubborn insolence'. Such influence did not avail when Harold's forces met William of Normandy at Hastings.

Wulstan was present in Westminster Abbey on Christmas Day 1066, when Harold's successor was crowned. That he survived the transfer of power testifies to how well he came to be regarded by the new King, who – William of Malmesbury tells us – found Wulstan's holiness, calm and unworldliness attractive. So much did he trust him that he engaged Wulstan to conduct a visitation of the Diocese of Chester and the three counties of Cheshire, Staffordshire and Shropshire at a time when these regions were 'so far off that the Normans had yet to come to them; on account of their barbarity, they were unsubdued'. Henry of Huntingdon describes how Wulstan would later show his absolute loyalty to the Norman regime, how he rejected Anglo-Saxon subversion and how there were limits to his saintly unworldliness. For in 1075 Wulstan and the Worcestershire *fyrd* countered the Revolt of the Earls against William the Conqueror while in 1088 Wulstan held Worcester for the new king, Rufus, against a violent uprising. He armed his tenants, animated the citizens, secured wives, children and moveables within the walls, organised a rigorous garrison defence, and then – when the besiegers attacked and burnt the suburbs - he ordered the garrison's counter-attack, which ended with some 500 rebels captured or killed at Wick south-east of the city.

Wulstan, then, had a rare talent for being able to combine effective and judicious political action on the national stage with a peaceable pastoral nature in his role as a churchman. This helps explain why he was held in such esteem, both in his lifetime and thereafter. Worcester flourished in his reflected glory, most visibly with the construction of a new cathedral church which was first used by the monks in 1089.

His death in 1095 was the occasion for 'great weeping and wailing'; he was buried in his new Cathedral, and the chronicler records that clergy and people equally felt the loss of a pastoral shepherd, teacher, wise man and miracle worker. Wulstan was celebrated and commemorated in religious houses across the country, but it was at Worcester that a cult was fostered. Twelfth-century monks appear to have encouraged what would be another lucrative tourist attraction, and the tomb was rebuilt and raised up above ground level; across time it suffered the attentions of pilgrims who chipped pieces off to keep as holy relics. That holy reputation was enhanced in 1113 when a devastating fire destroyed the Cathedral; Wulstan's tomb entirely escaped the blaze. When the same thing happened fifteen years later, a witness to the tomb's second miraculous survival, Bishop Bernard of St David's, petitioned Rome that Wulstan be canonised. But it was not until 1202, and further devastating fire damage, that progress was made in this regard. Bishop Mauger, aware of the need for re-building funds, and of the potential profit from another home-grown saint (in addition to Oswald), led petitioners on a journey to Rome to meet Pope Innocent III; the latter appointed a commission, which included the Archbishop of Canterbury, Hubert Walter. It concluded that the many miracles recorded at Wulstan's tomb were genuine. A group of Worcester monks led by Walter of Broadwas carried the archbishop's conclusions, with supporting letters to the Pope, on their own perilous trans-Alpine journey. And at last, in April 1203, a papal bull duly announced Wulstan's canonisation.

The crypt, the most complete surviving part of the Norman cathedral begun by Wulstan.

The Cathedral under Wulstan

Barely a century after the completion of Oswald's great cathedral church of St Mary, Wulstan ordered the laying of new foundations for another cathedral to be built on the site. Noake, the nineteenth-century historian, argued that Wulstan did so because Oswald's cathedral had been severely damaged by Harthacnut's soldiers, in revenge for the death of the king's housecarls back in 1041 (see Chapter 1).

Other historians have pointed to a trend after the Conquest for cathedral churches to be rebuilt on the grand Norman scale, in part as a statement about the power of the conquerors. It may well be that Wulstan felt obliged to conform to this, rather than being enthusiastic about the cause. His chronicler suggests as much, telling us that when the new building was well advanced the word was given that St

Mary's should be stripped of its roof and demolished. 'Wulstan stood in the open air and watched and could not keep back the tears'... (He said): 'We unfortunates are destroying the work of saints in order to win praise for ourselves. In that happy age men were incapable of building for display... But we strive to pile up stones while neglecting souls.' He sought to compensate for the destruction of Oswald's church by setting aside 70 marks to build a shrine to the saint.

That 'piling up of stones' did at least provide further proof of Wulstan's holiness, for William of Malmesbury related a miraculous tale of a labourer, climbing the ladders erected to build a new bell turret (one of Wulstan's enhancements to the priory church). He 'fell, but Wulstan was standing by and while the man was tumbling down he managed to get the cross between him and destruction. Not only was his body not broken but his mind was not stunned, and he arose unhurt.'

The speed with which the crypt, sanctuary and liturgical choir were constructed was remarked on by contemporaries and tells us something about Wulstan's organisational skills, as well as his extensive influence, for he drew on considerable manpower, and on a wealth of building materials from the Cotswolds and from the North.

The new cathedral church was consecrated in 1088. It consisted of choir, transepts, an aisled nave, and a great tower. The building's dimensions were not far short of those of the present cathedral. The crypt he built still stands and gives us an impression of the massive Romanesque building it lay beneath; so too does the beautiful chapter house, whose simple grandeur and innovative design make it one of the country's most important surviving Norman structures.

Like Oswald's cathedral church of St Mary, Wulstan's building did not last long intact. In 1113 the cathedral roof caught fire, the lead liquefied, and the interior of the church was badly damaged; in 1175 the Great Tower collapsed, even as two architecturally important bays of the nave were being commenced in the Transitional style. Further damage was caused by another conflagration in 1202. The cult of Wulstan now proved useful in generating the necessary income, first immediately to restore the cathedral, celebrated by King Henry III in 1218, and then to help pay for yet another rebuilding. This started with the Lady Chapel in 1224. Work on the new cathedral carried on intermittently over a period of 150 years, to culminate eventually in the great Gothic monument we still see commanding the River Severn.

CHAPTER 4
King John

King John is memorialised in the choir of Worcester Cathedral where his life-size effigy rests on a prominent stone tomb, flanked by Worcester's two saints, SS Oswald and Wulstan. He had visited the Cathedral in 1207 in the midst of a desperate struggle with the Pope, Innocent III, and had then committed himself to Wulstan's protection. In his will (which is held in the Worcester Cathedral Library) he instructed that 'my body be buried in the church of St Mary and St Wulstan'. Both tomb and testament reveal more about one of the most turbulent and disastrous reigns in English history than simply recording an attachment to Wulstan. That John's effigy is dressed out in full coronation regalia tells us that he understood the importance of putting on a show for his subjects; but it also reflects his vanity, his love of the trappings of power.

At the reality of exercising kingship he was much less successful; the drawn sword by his side speaks volumes about the continuous unrest which marked his rule. That last will and testament, written *in extremis* in his last days, calls on his faithful men (those who weren't part of a serious rebellion against the king) 'to provide support to my sons towards obtaining and defending their inheritance'. That John was buried at Worcester was not simply because of his fondness for Wulstan and the city, but because a Westminster burial, in a London firmly in the hands of rebel nobles and the French Dauphin, was an impossibility. The truth was that when he died he controlled only the western counties, and parts of the North and East Anglia; the capital, the south and south-east answered to a foreign prince and to many of the country's leading nobles. In seventeen fateful years John had managed to squander his vast inheritance and lose the Angevin Empire in France: Normandy, Brittany, Anjou, North Aquitaine. Only Gascony remained at his death. So, the inheritance for his sons, of which he spoke in his will, was much diminished; indeed, on his death in October 1216, it seemed very unlikely that his nine-year-old son Henry would succeed to the throne.

In the thirty-three years elapsing between his birth in 1166 and his succession in 1199, the youngest son of Henry II and Eleanor of Aquitaine had already proved arrogant, impetuous, volcanic, a poor judge of character, and thoroughly untrustworthy. Newly made Lord of Ireland in the 1180s, he swiftly managed to alienate the native nobility, foolishly relied on his callow favourites for advice, lacked the resilience to battle through difficulties, and hastily abandoned the country.

King John's burial. Bearers carry his coffin into the walled city of Worcester for burial at the Cathedral.

When his brother Richard I succeeded to the Angevin Empire on Henry II's death in 1189, John spent years plotting to replace him, even treasonably allying with the Empire's sworn enemy, the King of France, Philip Augustus. John promised Philip he would give up vital Norman lands in the Vexin between Rouen and Paris, in return for his recognition of John's succession to the Angevin lands; John was therefore prepared to barter away strategically critical territories. And when Richard was captured and imprisoned by the Emperor on his return journey from the Third Crusade, John negotiated to extend Richard's custody, to allow him to secure England in Richard's absence. Remarkably, the brothers were reconciled when Richard was eventually released, and after John had abased himself. By the time Richard died (1199) John seemed well placed to succeed him in an Empire stretching from the borders with Scotland, through Brittany and on down towards Spain and the Pyrenees.

He had lost most of it by 1204. At the outset, he faced his ambitious nephew, Arthur (son of John's deceased elder brother Geoffrey), who argued that his claims on the Empire were stronger than John's; he also had the misfortune to coincide with one of France's most able kings, Philip Augustus. The classical allusion was widely applied to a monarch whose martial success elevated and unified France. For from the time of John's father Henry II, Philip was relentless and single-minded in his aim of eradicating Angevin rule, the key to which was Normandy. He used his position as overlord of all French lands to encourage John's barons to appeal to him over John's head. He intrigued with young Arthur, backing his claim first to Anjou and then to the rest of Angevin lands. And although there were moments of negotiated peace between 1199 and 1204, or times when John appeared to have the upper hand, Philip's remorselessness won through. He was greatly helped by John's serial misjudgements, especially by his talent for making enemies. For example, his precipitate decision to divorce his first wife and marry Isabella of Angoulême (whose father held strategically valuable lands) not unnaturally alienated her intended, the powerful noble Hugh le Brun. Again, in the aftermath to a great martial triumph, the defeat and capture of Arthur at Mirebeau in Poitou (1202), he failed to reward William of Roches whose extraordinary personal courage and inspiring leadership had carried the issue. Finally, by having a captive Arthur quietly murdered in 1203, he drove many – who were appalled – into Philip's arms.

In 1204 the great citadel of Château Gaillard, constructed by Richard I on Normandy's borders as the key to its defences, submitted to Philip after a prolonged siege, at a time when John lingered in England. It precipitated the total collapse of Norman

Photograph by Mr. Christopher Guy, Worcester Cathedral Archaeologist. Reproduced by permission of the Chapter of Worcester Cathedral (U.K.)

King John's tomb in the Cathedral.

resistance to the French king, marked an end of England's historic link with Normandy and preceded the surrender of almost all other Angevin lands in France. Although John would fight back in 1206 in Gascony and Poitou, his failure to retaliate immediately in 1204 puzzled contemporaries, who variously concluded that he was too preoccupied with his young wife, that too many English barons were reluctant to follow him across the Channel to engage their French overlord, and that John feared treachery in England were he to travel to France. All explanations are plausible.

The loss of his continental possessions was a very serious blow to John; he lost access to vast revenues. As a result, his remaining lands in England and Ireland bore the brunt of his financial exactions, and the near universal opposition he faced by 1214/5 was exacerbated by his ingenuity and efficiency in gathering taxes from the hitherto exempt. In 1207, for example, he arbitrarily introduced the Thirteenth, a new tax on moveables and revenues, without waiting for the necessary agreement of the bishops; its yield (£57,000) was far higher than that from conventional taxes. He was equally resourceful in extending forest law, by which those impinging on the (extensive) royal forests could be fined heavily. Contemporaries worried that these taxes were forerunners to the extension of direct taxation. John's desperate need for money to fund the recovery of lost Norman lands also explains his enthusiastic sequestration of Church property from 1208. He discovered just how wealthy was the Church some 300 years before his Tudor successor. Still, the monks had their revenge; the unrelievedly black portrayal of the king that predominates in contemporary chronicles was their creation and reflected their perception of a tyrannical ruler.

The loss of an overseas Empire exacerbated his problems at home. Creative taxation upset many of the great men on whom a medieval king relied. His orders that they join him on an expedition to fight Philip placed many in a quandary because, strictly speaking, that would mean that they were fighting their French liege lord to whom they had paid homage. William Marshal, at the very heart of John's government, refused on just these grounds to set sail with an army from Porchester, bound for Poitou in 1205, occasioning the cancellation of the whole campaign. A hapless John embarked alone, circumnavigated the Isle of Wight, and returned humiliated. He and William Marshal were estranged for a period, and what this episode illustrates again was John's capacity to alienate friends and allies. The country's natural leaders were also suspicious of the way John at times appealed directly to their tenants in assemblies he convened all over the country.

No rupture was more spectacular than that with the Pope, Innocent III. It was prompted by disagreement over who should nominate a new Archbishop of Canterbury in succession to Hubert Walter, who died in 1205. John stood on his dignity and his rights, believing that the monarch should participate in selecting a successor. He quarrelled first with the monks of Canterbury who wanted their own candidate; at which point Innocent III appointed his own choice, Stephen Langton. John's refusal to accept this led to the country being placed under an interdict in 1208, effectively barring citizens from participation in religious ceremonies. From January 1209 John was personally excommunicated from the Church, a sentence to be 'solemnly repeated on successive Sundays and feast days with tolling of bells and candles lit'; among its consequences was the Church's encouragement for the King's subjects to depose him. By early 1213 John was seriously worried about a plot to overthrow him, centred both on Wales and in the North. As a result, he resolved to sue for peace, submitted to Innocent's terms, repented of his behaviour, and promised restitution of the church wealth he had plundered over five years.

Worcester churchmen played a central part in this long struggle between Church and State. In 1207 Innocent had instructed the bishops of London, Ely and Worcester to go to John to convince him to defer to the Pope's appointment of Stephen Langton. The following year Bishop Mauger of Worcester was one of the few English bishops to publish the Papal interdict, and fled the country to avoid John's wrath. But in 1212 Philip of Worcester was one of three senior figures sent to Rome to communicate John's submission to the Pope.

Although that submission disarmed Innocent, and made him subsequently a staunch supporter and ally, John encountered increasing opposition in England. His last throw of the dice, raising an army, and huge sums of money, to invade France (through La Rochelle) in 1214, had some initial success, but Philip Augustus's crushing defeat of John's allies, the Emperor Otto of Brunswick and the Count of Flanders, at the Battle of Bouvines in Flanders (July 1214), effectively scattered John's forces and left Philip in an unassailable position. Worse, John's military failure, and its cost, emboldened his enemies. By mid-1215 he was unable to gather taxes from many counties; his leading barons had taken London, had researched ancient charters and through their spokesman Stephen Langton were in a position to submit to the King's representatives at Runnymede (near Staines) their own charter confirming their liberties and limiting the King's arbitrary behaviour. This was Magna Carta.

With neither side trusting the other, hostilities resumed and the last year of his reign saw John embattled in Corfe while Louis, son of the King of France, was welcomed in London. Louis went on to lay siege to Dover, the key to controlling the Channel and the country's most important entry-point. Even Worcester was to disappoint John. He had taken a close interest in the city and in its famous Saxon saint since the start of his reign. It has been argued that John's trust in Wulstan (see chapters on SS Oswald and Wulstan for the emergence of cults around their relics after their death) was part of a much wider phenomenon whereby the upper tiers of society (still very much Continental Europeans) took an active interest in their Anglo-Saxon predecessors. As a consequence, he had personally ordered the rebuilding of fire-damaged Edgar Tower (the Priory's great gatehouse) in 1202 and had given 100 marks on a visit of 1207 to help rebuild the cathedral priory, which had also suffered in that same great fire of 1202. He was received there in solemn procession before praying at the shrine of St Wulstan in 1207. He had attended to the recruiting of Worcester men to fight overseas in 1205 and 1211. He held his Christmas court at Worcester on successive years in 1214 and 1215, while his troubles mounted in the rest of the kingdom. He enjoyed hunting in nearby Feckenham Forest. Yet at the end of his reign even in Worcester he found former loyalists rising against him. Valentine Green, the antiquarian, describes vividly in his *History of Worcester* (1796) how Worcester declared for the rebellious barons but how, months before his death, John's forces under Fawkes de Breauté overwhelmed the castle's defences just south of the Cathedral. He goes on to relate how the captured citizens 'were compelled by exquisite torture to discover their treasures', and how the convent was plundered and the gold gilding Wulstan's shrine was appropriated to be melted down to pay a heavy fine of 300 marks.

Worcester's temporary perfidy did not deter John from insisting on burial beside his favourite saint, in his will dictated at Lynn in October 1216. He left his young son, Henry, a seemingly impossible inheritance – rebel barons in the field, a foreign prince in control of the capital, and a much-diminished Empire. The loyalty of some key great men, William Marshal in particular; the swift concession of a more conciliatory Magna Carta in 1216 to assuage baronial feelings; an equally swift coronation of the young king at Gloucester – it was only the coincidence of these factors that permitted Henry III to succeed his father and begin the process of ridding England of the invader. Worcester had a further part to play in these years of Henry III's assumption of power. So weakened had the crown become, not helped by Henry's extreme youth, that the new king was forced to make the Treaty of Worcester in 1218 with Llewellyn the Great, leader of all the independent princes of Wales, by which Henry confirmed Llewellyn in all his extensive conquests, effectively leaving him free to rule Wales. The Treaty was a bleak coda to John's reign, one last consequence of a debilitating lack of statesmanship.

The serene majesty conveyed by the wonderfully realistic figure on his Worcester tomb is an artificial construct; those looking on it would not know that John's reign was an unmitigated disaster. But his personal failure did not prevent his becoming a commercial proposition in death; in the late 1220s an unseemly tug-of-war over John's remains occurred between Worcester's monks and the Cistercians of Beaulieu (John's religious foundation in the New Forest). Worcester's monks provided a tomb and effigy worthy of a king; they also skilfully played on Henry's awareness that his father had had great affection for the Priory and the city. They won the struggle to retain 'a valuable asset,' in the words of John's recent biographer, Stephen Church, and to attract 'vast sums of money into Worcester' for the building of its great Gothic cathedral. For their part the monks were careful stewards of a shrine to the King's memory up to the Reformation, one part of which was the singing twice daily for the next three hundred years or so of the *Laudes Regiae*.

CHAPTER 5

Prince Arthur

Worcester Cathedral features both in the prologue and the epilogue to the Wars of the Roses which scarred the country for twenty-five years towards the end of the fifteenth century. In Autumn 1459 the Duke of York and the Earl of Salisbury solemnly committed themselves, in an indenture signed and sealed in Worcester Cathedral, to support each other as part of their preparations for raising arms against Henry VI's evil counsellors, and against the king's failure to consult 'the great lords of his blood'. The Earl of Warwick then joined them a day or so later. A Yorkist conspiracy was in train. This would prove to be a preliminary manoeuvre before the onset of the First War of the Roses.

Yet the Cathedral's stonework also physically embodies Tudor statecraft as Henry VII sought to establish his dynasty on the English throne after his victory at Bosworth Field (1485), which was the culminating battle of those Wars of the Roses. For in a position of honour to the right of the high altar in Worcester Cathedral stands a magnificent example of late medieval masonry; this is the chantry chapel and final resting place of Prince Arthur, eldest son of Henry VII. Both its interior and exterior walls are replete with heraldic sculptures which tell us much about Arthur's life and significance. The white rose of York, the red rose of Lancaster, the composite Tudor rose, the eagle and fetter-lock (Yorkist emblems adopted by Henry VII), were carefully chosen symbols representing the Tudor king's policy of unifying a country riven for years by the bitter rivalries of the Wars of the Roses. Equally, the presence of the Welsh dragon, the white greyhound of Richmond, the Prince of Wales' ostrich feathers and the Beaufort portcullis, helped establish the Tudors' dynastic and regional connections, while the fleur de lis (from Arthur's great-grandmother, Katherine de Valois), the pomegranate of his widow, Katherine of Aragon, and the sheath of arrows, from Isabella of Castile, placed the prince in a wider European context. For in him Henry VII had vested all his hopes for the consolidation of the Tudor crown; Arthur's untimely death in 1502, at the age of fifteen, was a body blow to the king, and – by opening the way to Henry VIII's accession – transformed later English history.

When Edward IV died in 1483 his brother, Richard of Gloucester, moved swiftly to eliminate the old king's young son (Edward V) and took the throne for himself. Henry Tudor, Duke of Richmond, as heir to the Lancastrian cause, saw the opportunity to exploit the divisions in Yorkist ranks which Richard's usurpation opened up. Henry married Edward

Prince Arthur's chantry chapel, Worcester Cathedral.

IV's daughter, Elizabeth of York, a symbolic act of reconciliation between the two houses, Lancaster and York. Victory at Bosworth, and the slaying of Richard III, in 1485 ended the Wars of the Roses and brought Henry the throne, but he continued – not without cause – to feel insecure in the aftermath to the battle, being threatened by pretenders and by foreign invasion. Consequently, the birth of Arthur at Winchester in 1486 was both a matter of great celebration but, more than that, an event of huge importance in establishing a Tudor dynasty. Henry chose the birthplace and the name very deliberately; Arthur was named for the legendary king, that 'paragon of generosity, affluence, courage, military success and courtliness', recorded in the works of Malory and Geoffrey of Monmouth. The mythical

King Arthur had purportedly unified the kingdom against invaders. Associating the young Tudor prince with a British paragon, depicted in folk-lore as defeating Saxon invaders and then creating a British nation, was a calculated attempt to link the Tudors to a glorious, if invented, interlude in the country's history. At the time the extent to which this was merely fanciful history, almost entirely confected by the 12th-century chronicler Geoffrey of Monmouth, would not have been apparent.

Arthur was christened at Winchester, but just as Worcester marked the end of his life, so a bishop of Worcester, John Alcock, was significant in its beginning; he performed the christening in October 1486. From the outset the king saw this birth as part of his policy of reconciling rivals at the end of twenty-five years of bloody civil war. So, when it came to establishing Arthur's separate household in Ludlow from 1493 he entrusted those who had served the young Yorkist prince Edward V with the care and education of his infant son. And he surrounded Arthur both with his own loyalists and with others he now trusted to be true to the Tudor cause.

Ludlow Castle would be Arthur's home for the rest of his life. It was the centre of the Marcher lands – the Welsh Marches – encompassing Shrewsbury, Bewdley, Ludlow, Leominster, Hereford and Worcester, many of these forming the heartlands of the lordship of the Earls of March, the Mortimers. Queen Elizabeth, Henry VII's young Yorkist wife, was their most noteworthy descendant. The Mortimers had powerful claims to the throne through their ancestry to Edward III and so, in locating Arthur in the Marches, Henry was making explicit a strong family link to royal antecedents, as well as emphasising his own Welsh roots. It helped that the Mortimers, too, curated and broadcast their own connections to King Arthur and other legendary British figures.

Henry's aim was that Arthur, guided by carefully chosen loyalists, would gain an apprenticeship in governing far from the pressures, dangers and temptations of the court in London. Henry was also always mindful of the threat of an uprising which could see the whole family wiped out in one fell swoop; it was therefore important – if harsh – to separate his son from the rest of the royal family. In the Marches Arthur would be surrounded by people who held land, and were powerful figures, in the western counties; they could protect him. It helped both that he inherited strong structures (like the Council of the Marches) and precedents in the administration of the lands of the Earl of March, and that he was Prince of Wales, with all its impressive connotations. Here he would form a semi-independent principality, and Arthur would be slowly inducted in the ways of running his estates and dispensing justice; then, in the fullness of time, he would be capable of assuming national kingship, being thoroughly prepared for all the responsibilities which that role would involve.

He was educated as a Renaissance prince, becoming a skilled horseman and an able linguist. His command of Latin was such that he read Cicero and Quintilian in the original; through both he became familiar with political discourse, the construction of argument and the fundamentals of rhetoric and oratory, the command of which was essential for a self-respecting sixteenth-century monarch. Ambassadors and courtiers commented on Arthur's social ease and on his scholarship. Where evidence lacks is the extent to which he received military training; whether – for example – he practised in the tilt-yard to test his equestrian skills in practical exercises. However, given the importance of his role as viceroy in a large and strategically important part of the country, it is likely he was afforded tuition and practice in this regard in anticipation of future military engagement. What is certain is that although both Henry VII's sons were educated as befitted

Heritage Image Partnership Ltd / Alamy Stock Photo

The young Prince Arthur.

Renaissance princes, they could not have been more different in their upbringing. Arthur was brought up isolated from Whitehall's court life; his curriculum was carefully planned to nurture a serious-minded statesman familiar with administration and weighty policy decision-making. Young Prince Henry, five years younger, was given much

Heritage Image Partnership Ltd / Alamy Stock Photo

Prince Arthur's bride, Katherine of Aragon.

greater latitude, and many more social opportunities, especially with the female sex, by virtue of remaining with his parents at court. His education – perhaps short-sightedly, given the rate of mortality among teenagers in Tudor England – was not geared to his becoming king. His native impetuosity and wilfulness were not reined in.

So, it was naturally on Arthur that the heavy responsibility fell of making a success of an alliance with Spain, a keystone of Henry VII's diplomatic strategy. The arrangement would do much to secure international recognition of the Tudor house and elevate England's status by associating it with the dynamic and expansionist regime of one of Europe's newest colonial powers. Arthur's marriage to Katherine of Aragon, daughter of Ferdinand of Aragon and Isabella of Castile, was conducted by proxy at Tickenhill Place, Worcestershire, in 1499, two years before Katherine (aged sixteen) made the arduous journey from Corunna to Plymouth in late autumn 1501 for the marriage ceremonies proper. Henry had spent two years planning the practicalities of the event, opening up public spaces around St Paul's in London, constructing decking and platforms for wedding guests; this was an indication of the central importance of the event to his diplomatic strategy and to his plans for Arthur who would in time be joining the ranks of European monarchs and would by virtue of this marriage be impeccably connected. A contemporary account, *The Receyt of the Ladie Kateryne*, vividly recounts what transpired, detailing the ceremonials and the subsequent feasting and tournaments. Arthur's most recent biographer, Sean Cunningham, has dubbed it the 'Royal Wedding of the Century', such was its splendour and extravagance. Henry VII's conspicuous consumption and generosity in dispensing jewels to the Spanish ladies indicate his euphoria at the time and give the lie to his popular portrayal as tight-fisted.

What would – or would not – transpire on the wedding night in November 1501 has been the subject of intense speculation for five hundred years. It only became significant on Arthur's death. If Arthur is believed – 'Willoughby (steward of Henry's household), bring me a cup of ale, for I have been this night in the midst of Spain' – then the marriage was consummated. And the marriage the widowed Katherine later contracted with Arthur's brother, Henry VIII, would then founder on the impediment of affinity, by which close relations were barred by divine law from marrying. If Katherine is believed – that the marriage was never consummated – then her later marriage to Henry VIII could be seen as valid. These theological niceties mattered very much; Henry came to believe in the early 1520s that Katherine's inability to bear him a male heir was some sort of divine punishment for his transgression in marrying his brother's wife. Pope Clement VII's refusal to permit Henry to divorce Katherine set in motion a revolutionary train of events: a breach with Rome, the foundation of a Protestant Church and the destruction of the monasteries.

None of this would have happened had Arthur lived. But the young couple had only months together in Ludlow Castle before Arthur rapidly succumbed on 2 April 1502 to an illness whose nature has divided historians – was it tuberculosis or testicular cancer, or was it (the majority view) a bout of the very contagious sweating sickness, epidemics of which recurred in the last years of the fifteenth century? This was characterised firstly by cold and shivering, then by headaches and pains in the limbs, and finally by intense hot sweats accompanied by chest pain and delirium. From first indications to subsequent painful death was often only a matter of hours.

His death was shattering for his young bride marooned in a strange, cold and very foreign land. Equally it devastated his mother and father for in Arthur had been invested so many hopes and expectations. Now the dynasty was once again very vulnerable; the survival of the remaining son, Prince Henry, was yet more essential.

Although Ludlow had been his home and the administrative centre of his Marcher lordship, and although extensive funeral ceremonies took place there in early April, it was decided that Arthur would be most fittingly interred at Worcester, whose cathedral provided an edifice meet for a royal prince of such rare promise. Worcester's tradesmen were involved before the solemn procession accompanying Arthur's catafalque arrived from Ludlow, Cleobury Mortimer and Bewdley. For example, Thomas Billey of Worcester provided wax enough for the hundreds of tapers needed for the hearse and the graveside mourners. Gold and silver leaf and coloured paint were supplied by Worcester traders to decorate the hearse, banners and other accoutrements; they were worked by carpenters and painters and chandlers and metal-workers. They were sometimes directed by specialist painters and armourers from the Court; all engaged were contributing to a calculated manifestation of dynastic power, for it was important that the message that Tudor kingship had style and substance be reinforced. It was the more important because both Henry VII and Elizabeth stayed away, partly to underline that Arthur was a prince in his own right in his own lands, and also because the sweating sickness seems to have infected Worcester too. *The Receyt* records that all who could attend the funeral did so, 'savyng those of the cite because of the siknes that then reigned emonges them'.

On 25 April the procession arrived at Worcester from Bewdley. *The Receyt* gives a detailed account of the proceedings. The city friars met the procession at the north gate, and then fresh horses drew the hearse through streets lined with burgesses and commoners down to the Cathedral; here the vicar general of the absent Bishop of Worcester, accompanied by the staff and children of the cathedral community, met the cortège in the churchyard. The coffin was then borne through the cathedral close and on into a cathedral illuminated by 1068 lights, where it was carried up to the chancel. On the first night there was a service with the Magnificat and Benedictus sung in the Lady Chapel, and on the next morning large numbers reassembled to hear Masses of Our Lady, the Trinity and Requiem. Various heraldic ceremonies then culminated in a spectacular piece of theatre – one memorably recreated in 2002 in the Cathedral's service marking the 500th anniversary of the event – for Lord Gerald FitzGerald, Arthur's Man at Arms, rode the prince's horse down the aisle, to be received by the Abbot of Tewkesbury in the choir. Fitzgerald was wearing Arthur's full armour and carried his pole axe; the horse bore ceremonial trappings beautifully embroidered with Arthur's heraldic arms.

The emotional climax was reached with the laying of the prince's body in the grave, an event accompanied both by rising intensity in both the singing and the imprecations, and by an outbreak of weeping and wailing, with *The Receyt* opining that 'he had a hard heart that wept not'. After a series of offerings made to the coffin, after the dispensing of arms and the preaching of a sermon, anthems were sung by the congregation while the three bishops in

Prince Arthur's funeral at the Cathedral, reconstructed by local historian Pat Hughes.

attendance censed the coffin; at each *Kyrie Eleison* the cry went up 'for Prince Arthur's soul and the soul of all Christian souls, Pater Noster'. When at the culmination of the service the coffin was placed in the grave, the bishop of Lincoln, William Smith, who had so much to do with the young Arthur's education at Ludlow, offered up his own tearful prayers and the household officers broke their staffs of office and threw the pieces onto the coffin. This highly dramatic act symbolised the disbanding of Arthur's household and marked the tragic end of a promising life.

His early death is one of those events which prompts historians to ponder on what might have been. If Arthur had survived, or avoided the sickness, and lived on into adulthood, English history would have been very different. He and Katherine might well have had children to sustain the Tudor line. Prince Henry, Duke of York, would not have become king, to wreak havoc on the Catholic church and the religious houses. Given what we know of Arthur's temperament, England might well have avoided most of the wasteful wars to which his brother Henry later so willingly committed it. But of course, had Arthur survived to succeed Henry VII, he would have been buried in Westminster Abbey not Worcester, and that splendid late Gothic chantry chapel would not have seen the light of day.

The Early Modern Age

By permission of The King's School, Worcester

College Hall, King's School.

English history in the time of the Tudors and Stuarts was to a great extent shaped by two revolutions. The first stemmed from Henry VIII's break with Rome in the 1530s, the consequence of his frustrated efforts to divorce and re-marry, in the hope of securing his dynasty through a male succession. The king became supreme head of the Church in England. One immediate physical manifestation of this was the destruction of hundreds of religious houses in the dissolution of the monasteries – Henry needed their wealth to fund foreign adventures, but he also resented the adherence of many monks and nuns to the Pope in Rome.

For the next century English Catholics resisted the establishment of an Anglican (Protestant) church, sometimes by passive disobedience, but in Elizabeth's reign (and with Spanish help), through plots to remove her. The Gunpowder Plot in 1605, early in the reign of her successor James I, was the culmination of this. Almost as divisive were differences between Protestants as to the nature of the reformed faith which should be adopted in England: reformers wishing to retain bishops and an established church hierarchy were opposed by Puritans who favoured churches of the predestined elect, ministered to by pastors the congregation chose for itself. These disputes marred Elizabeth's reign; Charles I provoked much resentment among many Puritan gentry, by his encouragement of Archbishop Laud's religious policy which insisted on the re-introduction of altar rails, priestly vestments and other rituals, all of which smacked of Catholic practice; as a result many historians have seen religion as a proximate cause of the outbreak of Civil War in 1642.

A religious revolution which turned England upside down in the sixteenth century goes some way to explaining the second revolution of this Early Modern period: that of the king's subjects rising up against successive monarchs in the seventeenth century. Three civil wars between 1642 and 1651 were followed by the Interregnum and the Cromwellian Protectorate. Nor was the restoration of Charles II in 1660 the end of the upheaval, for such was the strength of feeling that his brother and successor James II provoked by his encouragement to the Catholic church, and by the threat he appeared to pose to the constitution, that he was driven from the throne in the Glorious Revolution of 1688/9 as his father had been before him.

The seven episodes which follow illustrate these predominant themes, starting with the dissolution of Worcester's famous Priory in 1539. Edward Winslow's daring expedition to the New World in 1620 is inexplicable without the context of contemporary repression of Puritan dissidents by the authorities; Thomas Tomkins's long life as director of music at the Cathedral in the first part of the seventeenth century was played out against a background of local Gunpowder plotters, of disputatious Calvinist and Arminian clergy, and later of a city and Cathedral precincts severely damaged by Parliamentary troops in the Civil Wars. Yet Worcester was quite evidently far from being the enthusiastic Royalist city of cavalier myth; the two chapters here on Worcester's central role in this period highlight the tensions between many Puritan tradesmen in the city and a strong Royalist faction of Dean and chapter, sustained by many large landowners from the surrounding countryside, some of whom still adhered to the Catholic faith. The influence of the latter ensured Worcester declared for the king, but the city was never wholehearted in its support.

Worcester also contributed to the story of the Glorious Revolution. James II's visit to the city in 1687 neatly exemplifies the growing gulf between the Catholic king and his subjects as he tried to impose his religious views on his people. In a Worcester-educated lawyer, John Somers, those who would resist the king's drift to autocracy found their champion. Through him Worcester can stake a claim to helping shape the Glorious Revolution which established the supremacy of Parliament and of Protestantism in England and Wales.

The medieval cloister, Worcester Cathedral.

CHAPTER 6
Dissolution and Renewal

The Cathedral Priory at Worcester was one of the glories of the late medieval Church in England. Its magnificent cathedral church, rearing up picturesquely on the banks of the Severn, formed the physical centre of a large diocese ministering to western counties. Because it was such a plum benefice its bishops were often absentee Italians rewarded with Worcester as an especially rich picking; one of these bishops, Giulio de Medici, became the future Pope Clement VII and had to contend with concurrent crises in the shape of the Lutheran Reformation, the assault of the Ottoman Turkish empire, and the sacking of Rome by Imperial forces. Worcester's prior in the last decades of the Priory's existence was William More, a well-known contemporary figure, whose importance to historians is the greater because of the chance survival of his Journal, a day-book which recorded his daily expenditure for seventeen years. It forms a unique and illuminating insight into the life and preoccupations of an early sixteenth-century religious house, and of its superior.

The key point is that he emerges from its pages as much more a wealthy country squire than as a religious figure. With his retinue of gentlemen – ten yeomen and ten grooms – his years were largely spent absent from the Worcester Priory, on his Battenhall, Crowle and Grimley estates, repairing, re-glazing and decorating the manor houses, stocking the fish stews, hunting, and administering the twenty-seven manors under his aegis. He entertained lavishly – at one stage hosting the young Princess Mary, the daughter of Henry VIII, for weeks on end – and spent freely, eating and drinking well, whilst also dispensing lavish largesse to the locals. There is no hint in his records of any premonition that this world was about to come to an end and that he would preside over the destruction of a whole way of life. For he was a steward of the kind of wealth which would attract the envious attention of a King and his faithful servant (Thomas Cromwell) as they searched for sources of income to subsidise expensive foreign wars.

Their policy of dissolving monasteries like Worcester's, which set in train one of the most revolutionary upheavals in all English history, was not the result of one single decision by Henry and his minister; instead a strategy emerged in the 1530s, hesitantly and gradually. The scale of destruction would be novel, but the principle had already been established. Some struggling lesser monasteries had been quietly suppressed and their resources directed elsewhere even before the 1520s when Cardinal Wolsey and his right-hand man, Thomas Cromwell, closed down a number of such houses to use the money to endow

Cardinal College, Oxford and a new school in Ipswich, Wolsey's home town. The next tranche of closures had taken place after a nation-wide visitation in 1535-6, by which government commissioners had investigated the state of numerous smaller foundations, paying particular attention to their moral tone and recording with some relish the sexual derelictions they found. They also issued to each house a set of injunctions, the full implementation of which would render the life of most monasteries absolutely impossible. These included strictly enforcing enclosure on every monk, abbots included – all were to be confined within the walls of the house at all times. Managing the estates would have been rendered impossible and one can only imagine how Prior More's life would have been constrained. The visitors' reports enabled Cromwell to close the delinquent lesser houses, and extract fines from those which pleaded for exemption from strict enclosure.

But Henry's break with Rome in the early 1530s had also provided a whole new imperative, for the Act of Supremacy involved an oath of supremacy to the king and the rejection of the Pope and of Rome – all traces of papal pretension to control the English Church were erased. It quickly became clear that loyalty to Rome persisted in some religious houses, and for Henry this was unacceptable. He found proof of such treason in the attachment of a few abbots and monks to the two northern rebellions (the Lincolnshire Rising and the Pilgrimage of Grace) in 1536 and that proof appears to have steeled the government to move from dissolving the lesser monasteries to moving on to tackle larger foundations like Worcester. Rebel northern abbots were executed, and their monasteries confiscated. As Cromwell said: 'The king is justly entitled by his laws thereunto upon this offence to have the whole moveable goods of the house'. Even in Worcestershire we find evidence of a reactionary attachment to Rome; in Pershore one monk, Richard Beely, reported to Cromwell how 'abbots, monks and priests do little or nothing to remove from books the Bishop of Rome's name'.

Worcester had had its own visitations already. The first was in 1526, when Cardinal Wolsey, hearing of Prior More's aristocratic lifestyle, and of some clergy who 'lead a life less honest than becomes them, to the ruin of their souls and the shame of religion', had sent a commissioner – Dr John Allen – to investigate. Allen concluded his inquiries with a demand for 'a new diligence' and a devotion in services to psalm singing. Then, in 1534 Archbishop Cranmer came to see Worcester for himself. He wrote of a lack of scripture reading (essential to the Protestant faith), of the Prior's reputation for lining his own pockets, of the fact that the Prior lived too well, and of its corollary, that the brothers were not always well fed themselves. In fact, Cranmer personified how much English religion had changed in just a few years. For now, with the king's breach with Rome,

World History Archive / Alamy Stock Photo

Hugh Latimer (*c.*1487- 1555), Bishop of Worcester, put to death by Mary I for his Protestant beliefs.

Protestant spirits were emboldened, none more so than Thomas Cromwell, Cranmer and the new Queen, Anne Boleyn. For them and for fellow reformers the easy-going monastic life of such as Prior More was anathema. Serious exposition of the Bible in the vernacular was all; superstition and all hints of Romanist practices were to be extirpated. Anne Boleyn's ascendancy at Court enabled her to advance a number of leading evangelicals, perhaps the most important of whom was Hugh Latimer – a firebrand of reform, scourge of superstitions, relics, saints, images, masses and monasticism, who would die for his beliefs as one of the Oxford Martyrs in 1555. Replacing another absentee, Italian Girolamo Ghinucci, he was appointed Bishop of Worcester in 1535, a nomination with national and international significance, for the Imperial ambassador wrote to the Holy Roman Emperor Charles V that Latimer's elevation to the see at Worcester 'was a great blow to the party of the old religion'.

On arrival in Worcester, Latimer immediately revealed a close interest in the spiritual and theological health of the Priory. He concluded his own visitation with: 'I perceive the ignorance and negligence of divers religious persons in this monastery to be intolerable; there doth reign idolatory and many superstitions (meaning pilgrimage to the reliquaries of St Oswald and St Wulstan).' As an antidote to such papist falsities he insisted that every monk must have a copy of the New Testament and attend daily lectures on the scriptures in English. It was the prescription of the authentic Lutheran radical.

A nationwide survey by his commissioners, the *Valor Ecclesiasticus*, furnished Thomas Cromwell with statistical evidence on the relative value of the remaining houses. Worcester's income was £1386, less than Canterbury (£1684) and the largest, Glastonbury (£3111), but even so it was in the top 4% of England's wealthiest monasteries. He then stumbled on a strategy for tackling these surviving foundations. It involved encouraging monks and others to denounce their superiors, and then using those condemnations as a lever to persuade abbots and priors voluntarily to surrender their houses to the Crown. The combination of the exemplary execution of those resisting the royal will (the Abbots of Glastonbury and Reading, for example), of moral pressure and of a kind of group psychology, as more and more joined the ranks of those submitting – all these explain the extraordinary speed by which the surrender of nearly 500 monastic foundations was effected in a couple of years. The process was over by 1540. And Worcester well exemplifies Cromwell's stratagem for – already no doubt feeling under pressure from Bishop Latimer – Prior More was faced with an accusation of treason made by a vengeful monk, John Musard. The latter had been a librarian at the Priory but had been dismissed for theft of plate. He wrote to Cromwell: 'As a religious man I am bound to send words of treason by my master', and alleged that More had protected another monk who had been overheard praising Queen Katherine of Aragon, and the Pope, and railing against the King and 'his whore', Anne Boleyn.

More avoided a treason trial. Friends at court who had sampled his hospitality ensured that he was allowed to retire quietly to live out his days in the comfort of the manor house at Crowle. But his successor was appointed on the understanding that the Priory be surrendered; it was handed over to the king in 1539, and in this bathetic way centuries of distinguished history were abruptly terminated. It was the same all over the country. The official instruction of the commissioners was 'to pull down to the ground all the walls of the churches, steeples, cloisters, fraters, dorters, and chapter houses,' and in a few years glorious buildings which had been the great beauty of the realm – their vaults, towers and spires, their chapels, their carvings, their choir stalls and their rood screens, their plate and their vestments – were destroyed or dispersed. A land transfer of perhaps a quarter of the country's estates was set in train; Worcester's Priory suffered less than most, the Cathedral, chapter house and College Hall surviving intact, but the properties of the city's friaries – Black and Grey Friars – and of the hospitals of St Oswald and St Wulstan, were also summarily seized, and a long history of medical care, education and hospitality was brought to an end.

So precipitately did the dissolution happen that there had not been time to develop a systematic plan for re-directing these assets. Henry claimed to be a Renaissance monarch, though his contribution to education and culture was up to 1539 etiolated. He had destroyed the disgraced Cardinal Wolsey's grammar school at Ipswich; he was on the verge of looting Wolsey's precious Cardinal (now Christ Church) College Oxford before being dissuaded. Now, in 1539 he was placed under considerable pressure to create a noble legacy with his new-found wealth; Worcester's very own Bishop Latimer, in a Lenten sermon at court that year, spoke of redistributing the wealth of the religious houses to centres of learning and preaching, rather than allowing it to fall to 'carnal gospellers' who just wanted to snare an abbey for themselves. 'Abbeys were (instead) ordained for the comfort of the poor'. That same theme we find reflected in a report in May 1539 to the French king Francis I by his ambassador, Marillac, where he recorded that the Commons were very exercised with the king and his ruinous war policy. He went on: 'the Commons are discussing the reduction of certain abbeys which they wish to make bishoprics, the foundation of schools for children, and hospitals for the poor'.

That King Henry was for once both stung and shamed we can deduce by the fact that on that very same afternoon legislation was hurried through the House empowering the king to endow new bishoprics from monastic revenue. In the preamble Henry wrote himself of his desire: 'that God's word be better set forth, that children be brought up in learning, clerks nourished in universities'. This then was the context for what happened in Worcester. Firstly, Worcester was one of eight pre-Reformation monastic cathedrals to be re-established as a secular foundation, not with monks but with a Dean and clergy supported by monastic revenues (although Henry, true to form, hamstrung the new foundation by applying only 25% of the Priory's income to the new establishment).

Secondly, Worcester would benefit educationally. It seems that the city already had a school (the antecedent of the Worcester Royal Grammar School) under the control of the guilds from as early as 1291. This city school emerged from the Priory which had long – since the days before Wulstan – provided schooling in its almonry where boys from the town could come for an education, a valuable training ground for parish priests. By the early sixteenth century there appears to have been teaching in the Priory once again, as well as in the city school, for the visitations of

Wolsey and Cranmer exposed a number of different concerns at Worcester's Priory. Wolsey's injunction that 'boys must be excluded from the monks' dormitories, chambers and private places' hints at an alarming moral laxity, while Cranmer's visitation betrays anxiety for the standard of instruction when it insisted that 'a resident should be employed in the monastery, a man of good character and sufficiently learned in the knowledge of grammar to instruct the younger monks'.

The decision to establish a King's school at Worcester – as at a number of newly secularised cathedrals, notably Canterbury, Ely, Rochester and Chester - was to be a further boon for the city's provision of education as well as for the surrounding county. At the very outset there was a debate as to who these schools were for; on the one side the odious Sir Richard Riche (head of the Court of Augmentations managing monastic property) argued that the schools should be just for gentlemen, not to be sullied 'by husbandmen's children fit only for the plough', while Thomas Cranmer believed the schools should educate 'poor men's children who were frequently more studious than those of gentlemen'. Certainly, at Worcester and at Canterbury that view pertained for at both the aim was to produce young men 'of piety and good letters to bear fruit for the glory of God and the adornment of the Commonwealth'.

Then, at King's Worcester, the new Master, John Pether, appointed by the King himself by Letters Patent in December 1541, was assigned to teach up to 40 King's scholars (Canterbury had 50; Chester and Ely 24) who were supposed to be 'poor and destitute of the help of friends and with an inborn aptitude for learning, as far as may be'. Yet despite the noble intentions, as is often the way, the ambitious middle classes rapidly colonised the school; the evidence is that early King's scholars often were not poor but were the sons of Worcestershire farmers, bailiffs, clergy and merchants, for a good education was a highly desirable commodity in a Tudor world of expanding employment prospects in law and government. Paradoxically, these new opportunities sprang from the economic revolution created by the Dissolution.

These King's scholars had four years to learn and speak Latin passably and in that time, they were to be maintained, boarded, taught and would receive their commons. They were based from 1544 in College Hall, the magnificent former refectory of the Cathedral Priory; and if that physical link to Henry VIII's original foundation still survives today, his endowment does not. Only a small number of the forty free places materialised, as Henry later pared back those monastic grants to the cathedral and the school which would have funded the foundation. Still, Worcester's King's School was one of few positive initiatives nationally which emerged from the broken cloisters and the bare ruined choirs, the poignant physical legacy of Henry VIII's religious policy.

CHAPTER 7

A Royal Progress and Worcester's Cloth Industry

Sixteenth-century Worcester was one of the wealthiest and fastest growing cities in the country. In terms of wealth it was one of the richest provincial towns in the middle of that century. Its population had expanded as births exceeded deaths, and through attracting immigrants from the surrounding counties. From approximately 4,250 souls in 1560 the population rose to about 8,000 by the end of the century. The growth in fact pre-dated the upheavals of the Reformation and the Dissolution which we have seen impacting on Worcester in 1540, and has been attributed by Alan Dyer 'to an upswing in the birth rate as reflected in the fertility of marriages', a feature from 1510 onwards. The city's new wealth was reflected in its buildings, with visitors commenting on 'fair, neat houses, most pleasantly seated'. William Camden, in his contemporary travelogue *Britannia*, believed that this new 'fame and reputation ariseth from the inhabitants, who are courteous and wealthy by the trade of clothing'. But in the first instance Worcester owed its prosperity to its advantageous location, for its bridge across the Severn conveyed travellers to South Wales and to the West; it also carried routes from Central Wales and the borders to London. Just as important was that position on the river which bore goods to the South (Tewkesbury, Gloucester and Bristol) and to the North (Bewdley, and then on to Bridgnorth). Downstream went cloth and wool and Droitwich salt, while Bristol supplied wine, fish oil, soap, iron and lead from the other direction. Henry VII's Star Chamber in 1504 confirmed Worcester's rights to levy tolls on wine travelling North, and on other goods passing the opposite way, and it flourished accordingly.

Its dominance of the region was reinforced by three other factors: it was the county town, hosting the assizes and the quarter sessions, and of course in so doing it accommodated and victualled the lawyers, the plaintiffs, and the gentry who sat on the bench. Worcester was the predominant diocese in the West Midlands and the Marches and the cathedral city was the centre of its administration. Finally, its fairs and markets were the means by which locally reared livestock (cattle, sheep and horses from areas to the West and North of the city) could be exchanged for cereals grown to the South and East, where the Vale of Evesham acted as the granary of Worcestershire. Luxury goods imported by mercers from London were sold in Worcester

The progresses of Elizabeth I around the country were substantial events. Legend has it that Elizabeth I stood on the balcony of this house to greet crowds when she visited Worcester.

to affluent merchants, clothiers and the local gentry.

That Worcester was growing and increasingly significant (it ranked sixteenth among England's towns and cities in the middle of the century) may be one reason why Elizabeth I decided to visit it on her progress of 1575. It may also be that Christopher Dighton, variously vintner, bailiff (senior civic leader) and Worcester's MP, used his influence in London to get Worcester included in her itinerary. Furthermore, it seems her interest was piqued by the presence of her uncle Arthur's tomb in the Cathedral.

Elizabeth's progresses were a mix of politics, entertainment and ceremonial. Firstly, they served a serious purpose in permitting her to project an image of regal power, allowing the nation to have access to their Queen and enabling her to learn about their local concerns. Equally, they were occasions for her to get to know her courtiers, her leading aristocracy and gentry, and to indulge in pageantry, pomp and ritual. Visits to cities and towns like Worcester, Coventry, Warwick and Woodstock, among other venues on her 1575 progress, were intended to boost civic pride. We are fortunate that the town clerk's official civic records, the *Chamber Order Book 1539-1601*, survive intact in the Worcestershire Record Office to provide a detailed account of Elizabeth's visit in August 1575.

Indeed, its narrative starts even before she appears, chronicling the instructions issued from the council chamber to direct that Worcester's four gates be 'sett in some decent color', i.e. repainted, 'that every person having donghills or myskyns (heaps of dung) shall cause the same to be carried away… shall clean their soyles and pave the same (in other words should clear up and repave the areas around their houses) and that every inhabitant within the liberties of this city shall whitlyme (whitewash) and colour their houses with comelye colours'. Similarly, the Grass Cross on Foregate Street and the cross at Sudbury (Sidbury) 'were to be sett in colours, together with the King's picture (statue of King John) at Sudbury gate'. There were detailed instructions for the city's ruling councillors: the two Bailiffs (Christopher Dighton was High Bailiff), Aldermen and High Chamberlain were to be dressed in scarlet and have their horses in readiness at Salt Lane End to meet her Majesty; and to bear their maces on horseback before her Majesty; of the rest of the ruling oligarchy, the Twenty-Four (members of the council) were to be apparelled in scarlet gowns faced with black satin, while the Forty-Eight (a further body of the council) would wear 'murrey' (purple-red, from mulberries) gowns. 'Every occupation by hym self in their gowns' would stand in serried order on the east side of the street holding streamers to signify their trade. The Master Bailiff was enjoined to inspect the livery gowns of every company; 'their brethren were to be comelye and decent'.

The account in the *Chamber Order Book* provides vivid detail of the Queen's visit. She rested at Hartlebury Castle, the Bishop of Worcester's residence, the night before, then rode in the late afternoon towards the city, stopping to alight at 'Whistons farme', there 'to attire herself' before riding on her palfrey to Salt Lane End at the top of Foregate Street. Here she met the Bailiffs, the city Masters, the Aldermen, gorgeous in their scarlet and black, the other mulberry-clad oligarchs, and the guildsmen representing the different occupations, displaying their distinctive streamers. By the time she had heard greetings, orations and obeisances, it was getting dark and her ride along Foregate Street towards the Grass Cross, and then the Cathedral, was rendered magical by the 'lights plentifully provided by the citizens at their doors, besides the garde (guard) and others carrying torches'. At the Cathedral porch the Bishop, Dean, prebendaries and choir in their surplices greeted the Queen and she entered the Church 'with great and solemn singing and music with cornets and sackbuts, with a canopy borne over her', progressing up to the chancel, 'where she diligently viewed the chapel and tomb of her dear uncle late prince Arthur, all richly and beautifully adorned'.

She made another visit to the Cathedral the next day, riding from the Bishop's Worcester palace in a coach, followed by the Earl of Leicester, other noblemen and women, and the maids of honour, all on horseback. 'The people being innumerable in the streets and churchyard crying to her Majesty 'God save your majesty,' she rose and 'shewed herself at both sides of her coach and often times said: 'I thank you all,' before proceeding into the Cathedral, through a line of the masters of the City standing in their scarlet gowns.' In the chancel again, next to Prince Arthur's chapel, she sat on a seat richly decked and adorned and 'herein a great and solemn noise of singing of service in the choir both by note and also playing with cornets and sackbuts' preceded a sermon by Dr Bullingham, the Bishop. The next few days were spent visiting city worthies and local gentry and were enlivened by hunting at Battenhall, and more successfully at Hallow Park where, 'with her bow she killed one buck'; from an elevation on Hynwykes Hill she viewed Pitchcroft, all the fields adjoining the city, and the Severn, right the way to Bredon Hill. When she came to depart she asked the Lord Bishop to commend her 'most heartily' to the Bailiffs of Worcester, and to their brethren and the whole city: 'I thank them heartily for their good entertainment… I like as well of them as I have liked of any people in all my progress, ye in all my life.'

Right to the end of what was seemingly a very happy visit Elizabeth was made aware that the city's leading citizens and advocates were anxious about their livelihoods. She learnt as much from an oration by Edward Bell made on behalf of the council soon after she arrived at Foregate Street on her first afternoon in the city; it accompanied the inevitable handsome and expensive presents, given by the worthies on behalf of the citizens to the Queen and her courtiers. After all the preliminaries, the thanks for past grants of charters by successive kings, and for her support for a free school which she had re-founded (the Grammar school) which would provide 'for the needy estate of Christ's poor members', he moved on to describe the fluctuating fortunes of Worcester's economy:

> This city of long time so increased in wealth, substance and beautiful buildings and became so fortunate in the trade of clothing that there were here used and maintained for the said trade of clothing 380 great looms, whereby 8,000 persons were well maintained in wealth and ability. Then flourished this city and became populous...but since this day your majesty shall see and find the wealth wasted and decayed, the beauty faded, the building ruinous. The looms are now 160 so that above 5,000 persons are now wanting; of all that was, there is almost nothing left but a ruinous city or decayed.

He went on to commend the action she had already taken to overturn the restraint of traffic, curbs resulting from legislation which his brethren believed had strangled trade. No longer would Worcester broadcloth pay heavier duties than those imposed on neighbouring Gloucestershire (and Wiltshire). Her initiative 'breedeth in us an assured hope shortly to see the restitution of our former flourishing estate'. And when the Lord Bishop spoke to the Queen on her departure he reiterated the city's message: 'It may please your majesty. So it is that their trade is not so good as it has been for the maintenance of their living, but their poor good wills and hearts your majesty has.' It seems clear that the Earl of Warwick who was accompanying her also took the message on board; he told the Master Bailiffs and the Aldermen that 'this is a proper city; it is a pity it should decay and become poor. For my part I will devise some way to do it good'.

Her distant successor, Charles II, was aware of the capacity and quality of Worcester's cloth industry when he brought his army to the city in 1651 for, through the good offices of the Mayor, he arranged for the clothiers to supply his men with their broadcloth uniforms of Red Tunic. It says something about the scale of the operation that the city was able to fulfil the order and fit out an army. He was defeated in the subsequent battle (see Chapter 11) and predictably defaulted on his debt of £453 3s. It was only in 2008, after correspondence between the surviving Company of Clothiers and Prince Charles, that another royal Charles came to Worcester, did the decent thing and settled the 350-year-old outstanding debt with a purse full of coin.

Tudor Worcester and the Cloth Industry

Worcester's population doubled in the course of the sixteenth century, and by 1600 it has been estimated at 8,000. It was not of course as large as London (70,000) or indeed as Norwich (13,000) or Bristol (10,000). What was notable was that such a large proportion of the population (c.50%) was engaged in one industry, cloth-making, and as a consequence Worcester was far more highly industrialised than most other Tudor provincial towns. Unlike other centres of English broadcloth manufacture, Worcester's industry was overwhelmingly urban, with the surrounding county largely excluded from involvement. It was dominated by small independent family operations in the city itself. Many Worcester households had spinning wheels, operated by women, especially apparently, by widows. Using the highest quality wool from the neighbouring counties of Herefordshire and Shropshire, whose proximity explains the siting of the industry here, they spun the yarn for the weavers, some of whom had more than one loom, others of whom were small-time capitalists running a number of looms in Worcester's larger houses, and operating additional looms in the homes of other clothiers.

The figure of 380 looms which Edward Bell quoted in his oration to the Queen is evidence of a very extensive industry, the more so as it has been calculated that the population was concentrated in some 930 households. Many Worcester houses would therefore have been furnished with a loom. Its product was the very highest quality broadcloth. The city's 500 cloths annually compared well with that of the much larger city of Norwich, which averaged 557 cloths per annum. The great majority of Worcester's cloths were sent to London for sale, while some of the cloths were marketed by Worcester merchants who grew rich on the business.

A visitor to Tudor Worcester would have encountered the evidence of the cloth industry at every turn: spinning wheels in the parlours, looms in the work-rooms, and the gardens and back yards where fullers, in Worcester known as walkers, washed, cleaned, milled, thickened and beat the cloth to shrink it before cutting it. Their handiwork would have been visible as the broadcloth hung on drying racks. One area in particular was known for these fulling racks, that of Black Friars, the grounds of the dissolved friary close to the north walls of the city. Because no significant dyeing industry developed in Worcester, right up to the seventeenth century the city was famed for its white, undyed broadcloth, rolls of which were laid for the visiting James II in 1687 – (see Chapter 12).

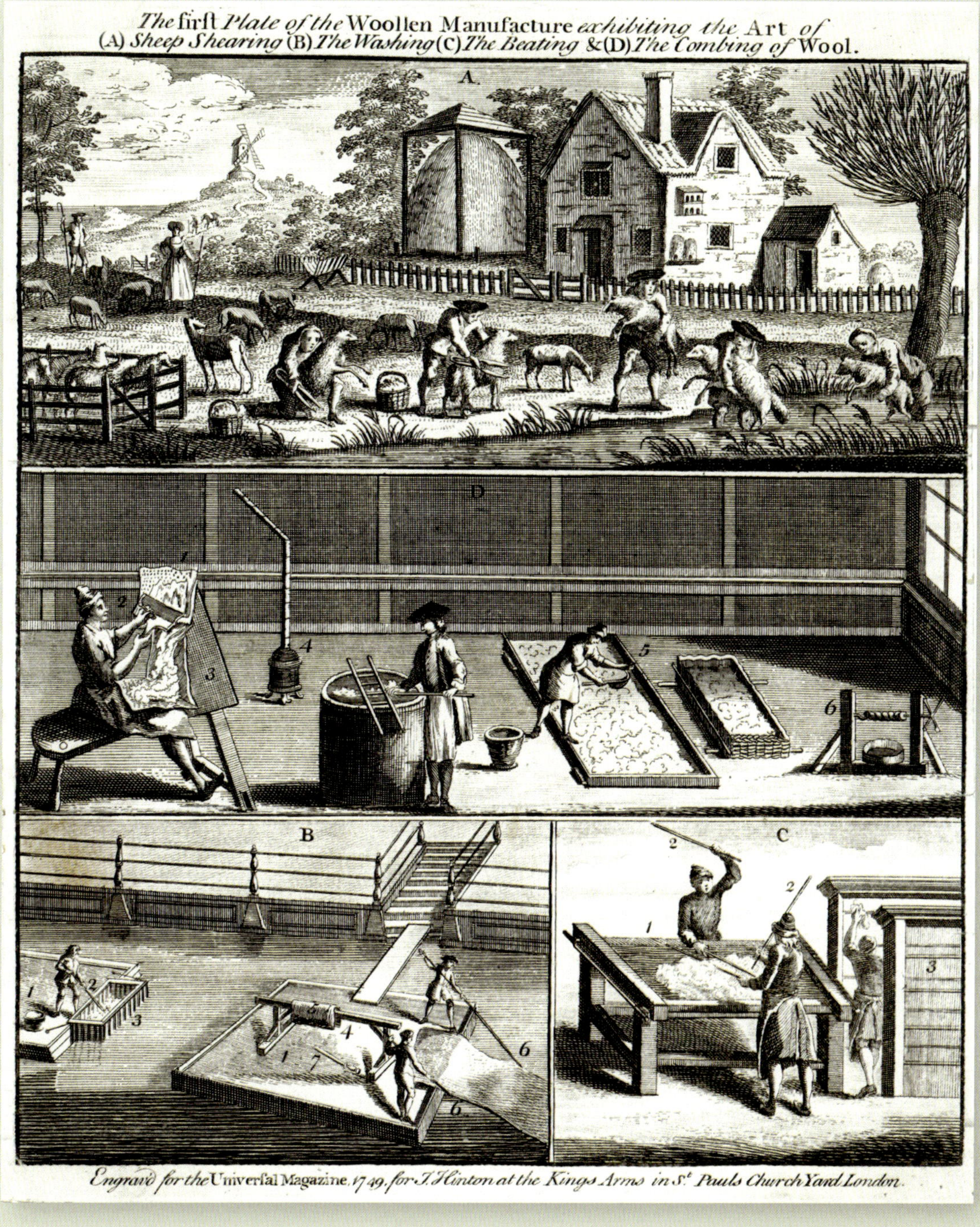

This 18th-century illustration shows the ancient processes within the wool industry that were so vital to Worcester's prosperity.

CHAPTER 8

Thomas Tomkins – A Concordant Composer for Discordant Times

Worcester's Thomas Tomkins is remarkable in a number of ways. For sixty years he was the Cathedral's organist and choir-master, establishing a national reputation; at the same time he was one of the country's leading composers of both secular and religious music in what some musicologists have called 'the golden age of English music'. He was preeminent in the late Elizabethan/early Jacobean school of madrigal writing, while his sacred verse anthems are now recognised for their technical brilliance. He learnt his craft in the last years of Queen Elizabeth and was evidently taught at this time by the great William Byrd, to whom he dedicated a song with the words 'To my ancient and much reverenced master'. Fifty years later, however, he would end his days in exile outside Worcester, one of thousands to suffer the depredations of the victorious Parliamentary forces. The national events that touched him at Worcester over the course of half a century are just as instructive as his musical career.

Born at St David's in Pembrokeshire in 1572, Thomas Tomkins was the son of another Thomas, who was a vicar choral at St David's Cathedral. He fathered a family of musicians, for the young Thomas's three half-brothers all became prominent, with both John and Giles serving at different times as organist of King's College Cambridge. Thomas junior learnt his musical craft in St David's, where he was a member of the cathedral choir, and in Gloucester to where his father moved on his appointment as a minor canon in the cathedral. It seems likely that it was in Gloucester that Thomas junior studied under William Byrd. Tomkins' biographers have surmised that it was through Byrd that Tomkins was introduced to the Chapel Royal as a gentleman of the Chapel. The Chapel Royal was part of the royal household, consisting of priests and musicians who travelled with the monarch, serving the spiritual needs of the monarch and the royal household; a part of this was the performance of a choral liturgical service. The music and the singing there were outstanding, and the historian Anthony Boden cites the opinion of the French ambassador who averred that 'in all my travels in France, Italy and Spain I never heard the like… a concert of music so excellent and sweet as cannot be expressed'. That quality reflected the Queen's own love of

By permission of The King's School, Worcester

Thomas Tomkins' home on College Green, Worcester.

music; she herself was a very capable performer on the lyre and the virginals, and it is no overstatement to say that only her interest in, and patronage of, church music saved the Anglican Church from the worst strictures of Puritans, who had no love of music, too reminiscent of the old Catholic ways.

We do not have precise dates for all the landmarks in Tomkins' early career, but it seems clear that he spent many years at the Chapel Royal, becoming a Gentleman Ordinary in 1621 and an organist there under his friend, the senior organist Orlando Gibbons, whom he succeeded in 1625. All this time he was establishing a reputation as a composer; in the closing years of Elizabeth's reign he had evidently made enough of a mark to be included in Thomas Morley's famous anthology, *The Triumphs of Oriana*, a collection of twenty-five madrigals in praise of the Queen, to which Tomkins contributed *The fauns and satyrs tripping*.

Yet Tomkins was in one sense leading a double life for, in 1596, he took up the position of master of choristers at Worcester cathedral, a post he would hold until his death in 1656. While his careers at court and back in Worcester continued for years in parallel, to an extent they represent two aspects of his musical contribution. The courtier in him will have responded to the challenge of writing secular madrigals, poems and lyrics set to polyphonic music, which is a composition made up of a number of parts, sung by different voices harmonising with each other. From Italian Renaissance origins they had developed by 1600 as complex, virtuosic displays by composer and singers, and were the forerunner to modern opera. They were at this time very much the height of courtly fashion. These and other songs were published in 1622 and represent the swansong of a brilliant period of madrigal composition. Robert Hollingworth, a foremost modern interpreter and performer of Early English music, has described the *Songs of 3.4.5. and 6. Parts* (1622) as 'unique for a book of mostly English madrigals in its unremitting quality and breadth of invention. Not only is every piece very fine, but many are outright masterworks.' Rather as Elgar would do in his *Enigma Variations*, nearly three centuries later, Tomkins dedicated each song to a different friend.

On the other hand, the challenge of developing a programme of religious music for his Cathedral choir at Worcester made of Tomkins a prolific composer of full and verse anthems, amongst which *When David Heard* is an acknowledged masterpiece, admired at the time for its 'exquisite invention, wit and art', the acme of Tomkins' command of polyphony and counterpoint. Years after Thomas Tomkins' death his son Nathaniel, another fine musician, would collect his father's sacred works together in *Musica Deo Sacra*, which comprised five services, five psalm tunes, the Preces, two proper psalms and ninety-four anthems, representing in total forty-five years of composition. For Thomas Tomkins this was the most important work he did.

This division of court and cathedral, secular and religious, was not of course absolute, and it seems that Tomkins, first as a Gentleman Extraordinary, then as a Gentleman Ordinary and an organist, was called increasingly to express the Court's joy and grief through the medium of sacred music. He had composed *O grant the King a long life* for James I's coronation, probably for use in Worcester's cathedral. But in 1612 the death through typhoid of Prince Henry, King James' elder son, was a heavy blow to the whole country and above all to his father. Tomkins was one of a number who wrote anthems for the prince's funeral, his fine composition *Know ye not*, being his contribution. Thirteen years later in 1625, when James himself died, it fell to Tomkins to compose the music for two successive royal occasions, James' funeral and the coronation of his son, Charles. These were exhausting times for Tomkins and the musicians of the Chapel Royal. Prior to the funeral a contemporary account tells us that:

> Two days before the day of the funeral the corpse was brought into the said Chapel in great solemnity with an anthem, and set upon the hearse of velvet, and the

> gentlemen of the Chapel from that time waited there, and performed solemn service with the organs brought thither for the purpose; they also waited with the corpse by day and night; by night first the decani side, and next cantoris side and twice in the night they had prayers… and ended with an anthem.

No sooner was the funeral over than Charles rushed down to Dover to greet his new bride, Henrietta Maria. Charles corralled a large retinue at Canterbury to provide a fitting welcoming party. The entire Chapel Royal with its vestments and plate and music and books had to be transported to Canterbury Cathedral, there to perform in a service designed to impress the new Queen and her train. All this upheaval was too much for Orlando Gibbons who suffered a catastrophic stroke; now it was Thomas Tomkins' sole responsibility to compose the eight anthems for the new king's six-hour coronation – amongst which are preserved *Behold, O God our Defender* and *Sadock the Priest* – and then to rehearse them. It was, according to Boden, 'the single most important event of his entire career'.

It might be expected that Tomkins would gain preferment after his heroic efforts, but he was to suffer mortifying disappointment. Firstly, he was raised to the most important musical post at court, that of Composer-in-Ordinary; and then, in farcical circumstances, it emerged that as a result of Court intrigue the post had already been promised to the son of Alfonso Ferrobosco, his predecessor, and that therefore Tomkins would have to surrender the position. This evidence of the new king's faithlessness did not prevent Tomkins from remaining an ardent Royalist in years to come, but still, it was a galling episode and increasingly he spent less time at Court and more back in Worcester.

Life there was no freer of intrigue than it was at Court, and indeed across Tomkins' sixty years in Worcester it became a good deal more dangerous. In the first years of King James the city and the surrounding county were much involved in the Gunpowder Plot, (see below). A number of prominent families in the county were Catholic and lived on estates which ringed Worcester. Tomkins could have been in the large crowd witnessing the bloody aftermath to the plot, the multiple executions on Red Hill, but more likely he was elsewhere in the city at the time.

The twenty years after the plot were quiet and reasonably harmonious ones for the country; and in Worcester the confidence which peace brought was expressed in 1612 by the building of one of the finest cathedral organs in England by Thomas Dallam, the foremost organ-builder of his generation. Thomas Tomkins had campaigned for it; the Cathedral's music and the musician himself greatly benefited from it. It was much admired, notably by the future Archbishop of Canterbury, William Laud.

This same Archbishop Laud would later pursue an extremely divisive religious policy, with the complete support of his king, Charles I. Tomkins' own cathedral at Worcester suffered from the very same controversies that Laud provoked all over England and Scotland by his insistence on elaborate ritual and services, on the sacrosanctity of the altar and of the ceremonies attached to the eucharist. Worcester was riven between a faction led by the dean and by Nathaniel, Tomkins' own son, who was prebendary and a minor cathedral canon; they were Laudians. On the other side were the bishop and the townspeople. The town council paid for a weekly visiting lecturer, and for the special seating to accommodate a large audience in the Cathedral; these signs of Puritanism, of belief in the efficacy of the pulpit and of faith in the Word were anathema to Laudians and a long and bitter struggle ensued lasting up to the first Civil War. Tomkins sympathised with Laud and his support for ceremonial, for vestments and for a touch of religious theatre; Laud was also a man of genuine musical sensibility. This explains why one of Tomkins' most important and beautiful compositions comes late in his life when he wrote *Pavan: Lord Canterbury*, a tombeau or homage in memory of a friend, executed by Parliament for his religious policy and for his closeness to the king. He would write another tribute, *Pavan: Earl Strafford*, for the fallen favourite Thomas Wentworth, the king's hated chief minister. Tomkins' Royalist sympathies could not be clearer. Not that they did him much good when war broke out in 1642.

After the battle at Powick in 1642 (see Chapter 10) the city was occupied by Parliamentary forces. As William Dugdale recorded:

> The whole army, under the command of the Earl of Essex, came to Worcester (and) the first thing they there did was the profanation of the cathedral: destroying the organ, breaking in pieces divers beautiful windows, and barbarously defacing divers fair monuments of the dead.

Organ pipes were wrenched out and thrown to the ground in such a frenzy of righteous fury that one Parliamentary vandal lost his footing and fell from the screen to his death, breaking his neck in the process. Although Essex's forces withdrew, it then seemed wise to dismantle the organ for safe-keeping.

A year later those forces, now under General Waller, encircled the city and bombarded it with cannon. Tomkins' large house on College Green, which he had built in 1628, took a direct hit. The Cathedral records chronicle subsequent payments 'to the Mason for tiles, lime and work done in reparation of Mr Organist's house, ruined by cannon shot when Waller attempted the taking of the city, May 29 1643'. And although on this occasion the Royalists held out, they were to succumb in 1646 after the prolonged siege of Worcester. The city was occupied by an army hostile to bishops, church establishments and to cathedral music. The choir was disbanded, the cathedral church locked and bolted. And Tomkins was forced to turn to composition; it was now that those beautiful tributes to Laud and Strafford were written. In 1649 the execution of the king prompted him to compose the superb *Sad Pavan: for these distracted times*, a keyboard piece of great simplicity, unity and intensity. These 'distracted times' affected Tomkins personally too, for his known Royalist sympathies brought him to the attention of Parliamentary inquisitions which determined the sequestration of Royalist estates.

Because he was well liked the Mayor and Aldermen of Worcester interceded on his behalf with the Committee for Compounding which determined fines for Royalists:

> We, the Mayor and Aldermen of the city of Worcester do... certify that Thomas Tomkins... being of the age of 78 years, has lived here very near 60 years. Always reputed an honest quiet peaceable man, conformable to all orders and ordinances of Parliament, and ever since the troubles began has had his constant abiding with us.

This was such 'an honest quiet peaceable man' that in his direst extremity, when Worcester was at the centre of another conflict in 1651 (see Chapter 11) and he was forced finally to leave the city, he still found money to put aside for the poor of Worcester.

He retired to Martin Hussingtree, a village on the Worcester to Droitwich road where his son Nathaniel's new wife Isabella owned a manor and was able to give him a home. In gratitude Thomas composed the charming *Galliard, The Lady Folliot's* in her honour. He died in the exceptional heat of May and June 1656 and was buried in Martin Hussingtree churchyard. He did not live to see the Restoration or the revival of Worcester Cathedral's services in August 1660, soon to be conducted by his nephew, Giles Tomkins, heir to a great family musical tradition.

Thomas Tomkins' reputation has risen and fallen in the past three-and-a-half centuries; the great foresight of his son Nathaniel to collect his *Musica Deo Sacra* and his own publication of his songs in 1622 have enabled musicians in the twenty-first century specialising in Early English music to rehabilitate him and establish him as one of the foremost composers of a Golden Age which bridged the period between the death of William Byrd and the emergence of Henry Purcell.

Worcester and the Gunpowder Plot

Worcestershire and neighbouring Warwickshire were homes to some of the most prominent Catholic gentry in England; a number of Catholic estates surrounded the city of Worcester, and several of their owners were associated with Guy Fawkes' Gunpowder Plot in 1605, a desperate attempt to blow up Parliament and bring about a Catholic revolution in England. Among these were the Wintour brothers (Thomas and Robert) of Huddington Court, six miles from Worcester, to where the plotters fled after the thwarting of the plot in November 1605, before they journeyed on to Holbeche House in Staffordshire, where a number of the Plot's leaders were cornered and killed or captured.

Humphrey Packington's Harvington Hall at Chaddesley Corbett, a few miles north of the city was riddled with priest holes to protect Catholic sympathisers. Closest of all was Hindlip Hall, right on the city's edge to its north-east. The home of Thomas Abington, Hindlip's multiple priest holes gave sanctuary to several highly sought-after Catholics in the months following the plot. Among them were Edward Oldcorne, Nicholas Owen, Ralph Ashley and Henry Garnet. Henry Garnet was the head of the Jesuits in England; he trained and encouraged Catholic priests in the last years of Queen Elizabeth's reign, and maintained a secret press to produce pamphlets to sustain a country-wide Catholic following. In January 1606 he and the two other Jesuit priests, Oldcorne and Ashley, were captured at Hindlip, after an intensive search of eleven days, along with Nicholas Owen, the most famous, most ingenious constructor of priest holes in England. Garnet and Owen had long been the foremost quarries of government authorities seeking out the Catholic leaders. While Garnet faced trial and execution in London and Owen died in the Tower after prolonged torture, Oldcorne, Ashley, John Wintour and several others were taken to Red Hill outside Worcester's walls to the south-east. There they were summarily hanged, drawn and quartered. Thomas Abington, owner of Hindlip, had also been condemned but was eventually reprieved because he had no part in the Plot itself. His punishment was that he should never again set foot outside Worcestershire, a condition he rigorously observed to the extent that on one occasion, as part of his research for a definitive work on Worcestershire parishes, he visited Tardebigge Church, which straddled the county boundary; he scrupulously avoided entering the chancel, because it lay in Warwickshire, instead noting its monuments at a safe distance from the nave.

Worcestershire Archive and Archaeology Service

16th-century Hindlip Hall, home to one of Worcestershire's strongly Catholic families.

CHAPTER 9

Edward Winslow and the New World

Worcester gave its name to the second most populous town in Massachusetts, which was permanently settled in 1722. This was fitting for a century earlier, one of its sons had been a prominent Pilgrim Father. Edward Winslow was one of the acknowledged leaders of the *Mayflower* pioneers, whose diplomatic skills and deep understanding of – and sympathy for – Indian language and culture made him a significant figure in the history both of Plymouth and Massachusetts.

Born in Droitwich in 1595, the son of an aspiring merchant who specialised in grain, pease and salt, Edward was evidently academically gifted, with 'an inborn aptitude for learning' and won a scholarship to the King's School in Worcester. His headmaster, Henry Bright, had a profound influence on him, as he had on many of that generation. Edward Winslow became an accomplished linguist; it does not seem fanciful to suggest that his interest – and later fluency – in North American native Indian languages stemmed from his proficiency in classical languages. Bright had a still more pervasive influence; a powerful preacher of a largely Puritan theology, he reinforced Winslow's familial Protestantism.

Although Edward would leave Worcester for London in 1611, and then for greater adventures in Holland and America, his education there had been formative, and he never forgot it. Indeed, after a printing apprenticeship in St Bride's where he worked on Puritan tracts, he left for Leiden in Holland to work for another alumnus of Worcester's King's School, Thomas Brewer, one of the most notorious Puritan activists of his day. By leaving for Leiden, centre of the largest printing industry in Europe, a magnet for Protestant intellectuals and a refuge for religious exiles from England, Winslow became an outlaw. James I, as later his son Charles I, believed Puritan sects, with their rejection of bishops and Anglican discipline, to be deeply subversive. In printing the writings of exiled Puritan divines Winslow was engaged in an illegal activity.

Winslow joined a Leiden independent church (that of the Scrooby community, exiled from Nottinghamshire) led by the brilliant Puritan preacher John Robinson, but by 1619 its ability to meet and worship was being compromised. One of the conditions James I extracted for supporting the Dutch in their ongoing struggle against the Spanish was that the authorities should clamp down on these independent church communities, and on the printing activities of English Puritan exiles. Difficulties in Leiden hastened a decision to seek a new life in America, far from government control. Edward Winslow was moved to

Pictorial Press Ltd / Alamy Stock Photo

This painting by Jean Leon Gerome Ferris imagines the signing of the 'Mayflower Compact' in 1620. Winslow stands behind the table, holding the ink.

participate by Utopian ideas of founding the new Jerusalem, as well as by visions of an anti-Catholic crusade and of propagating the gospel.

He was one of an intrepid 102 souls who embarked from Southampton in the *Mayflower* in 1620 on a perilous crossing to the New World. Many of those who survived the storms succumbed that first winter on American soil when, ill-prepared and cold, hungry and prey to illness, they clung to the narrow littoral strip of their new Plymouth colony. Over fifty colonists died in the first three months, among them Edward's first wife, Elizabeth, whom he had married in Leiden. He later married Susanna White, the widow of a fellow colonist, this being the first marriage in Plymouth's history. Within years Edward had acquired considerable land (800 to 1,000 acres), had founded a town – Marshfield – and had built a large house, which he named Careswell, after his Worcestershire family house; fertile, and blessed with a wealth of fish, fowl and fruit (even imported pear trees from his native Worcestershire), it became an almost Edenic life.

Beyond simply surviving and putting down roots Edward Winslow was notable as one of the most articulate, and cerebral, of the settlers; he was a leading light in the drafting of the 'Mayflower Compact', a founding constitution which bound the adult males 'to observe just and equal laws'. It has been claimed that Plymouth Colony was the very first experiment in the West, since classical times, in consensual government – an agreement of individuals one with one another, rather than with a monarch. Winslow was also the first, and most important, English settler in Plymouth to develop close relations with the local Indian chief, Massasoit, Sachem (leader) of the Pokanoket tribe; their subsequent enduring friendship was critical to the establishment and survival of the tiny English community.

Winslow's anthropological interest in the Indians, and his emerging friendship with Massasoit – sealed when Winslow nursed him when seriously ill – was expressed in an important written account, *Mourt's Relation*, (1622), the first of the Pilgrim Fathers' communications with England. Aside from describing Indian life, *Mourt's Relation* contains the first known description of the Thanksgiving celebrations. In this and his later work, *Good News from New England*, Winslow expressed an unfashionable compassion for the Indians, regarding them not as inferior savages but as equals. He recorded their customs, their behaviour, and the rich flora and fauna of their lands; he also sought to convey their attributes and their strict code of morality. It seemed that the English colonists had stumbled on a paradisical idyll, but not all Indians would be as accommodating or peaceable as Massasoit. Winslow's initial sympathies with the Indians reflected a feeling among many colonists in these early years that the native peoples were not savages, but that English and Indian societies were equivalent; English society was not seen as superior. In time this tolerance and understanding would be replaced by a hard-headed realism which came to justify violence, and even massacre, as a necessary means to survival.

Indeed, Winslow himself was persuaded into a much more proactive and aggressive policy as relations deteriorated, largely caused by the settlers' steady expansion into Indian territories. He was instrumental in the decision – made on the advice of his friend Massasoit – to forestall plots by other Indian tribes, by trapping and killing their leaders in 1623. 'If God had let them loose they might easily have swallowed us up,' he said. Nor did he object over a decade later when his Massachusetts friends unleashed a terrible slaughter on the Pequot tribe which was deemed to be a danger to the colony. That genocide, for not even women and children were spared the massacre, coloured all future relations between colonist and Indian in New England, culminating as it did with the bloody retribution of the Indian uprising in the 1670s, long after Winslow was dead. Thus, in

Winslow there were opposed two strains – a deep sympathy and understanding for Indian culture and society, warring with a pragmatic and rational recognition that Indian opposition to English settlement on its historic lands presented a systemic threat to its very existence.

Winslow was equally important in developing Plymouth trade. In time as a factor he would also represent neighbouring Massachusetts, a larger colony which he admired. He was the first Pilgrim Father to return to the mother country, bearing beaver and otter skins, as well as timber which was invaluable for masts for the Navy. And he was the preeminent Plymouth pioneer in the new country, guided by Massasoit's braves to explore the coast of East Maine and inland forests and rivers. Later he would travel up the Kennebec River to Hudson Bay and negotiate over fur supplies with the northern tribes. He was also the first Englishman to see the 400-mile stretch of water called Quinetucket (Connecticut), establishing a trading house with Connecticut Indians, which brought Plymouth into conflict with the Narragansett Indians who considered Connecticut to be their rightful province.

Winslow was multi-lingual; that and his even temperament, which made him a talented diplomat, established his reputation as the principal go-between for Plymouth colony with the Indians. Those diplomatic skills were equally invaluable back in England. Trips there were not simply for trade; just as important were, firstly, a financial imperative, for Winslow was the colony's chief negotiator with the Merchant Adventurers who initially backed the *Mayflower* expedition. He was central, too, to the subsequent re-scheduling of colony finances in London. Secondly, he had to face down English critics of the colonists; with Archbishop Laud imposing his prescriptive form of Anglicanism on the English Church, the Plymouth colonists seemed ungodly to many. After all, the Pilgrims had no Anglican priest. As a consequence, marriages were conducted by laymen like Edward, and this infraction got him – briefly – arrested on a visit to London in 1633, until an old Worcestershire family friend, Lord Coventry, intervened to release him.

In other regards too, Winslow was the most persuasive advocate for the New England colonies. This required stamina, for he was still wrestling into the mid-1640s with interfering politicians who wanted to regularise Massachusetts and Plymouth affairs by bringing them under Parliamentary governance. Edward powerfully argued that the New World colonists had come into existence to flee those self-same meddlesome spirits. Fortunately, at the end of the First English Civil War, many politicians on the ascendant Parliamentary side were – like Oliver Cromwell himself – Independents, who disapproved of any ecclesiastical discipline which had echoes of the Anglican regime they had fought to overcome; Plymouth and Massachusetts were eventually spared close

Parliamentary scrutiny.

Edward Winslow was successively governor of Plymouth colony in 1633, 1636 and 1644. He represented Plymouth and Massachusetts in diplomatic missions; he was the architect of an early federalising of the infant New England colonies, devising first the New England Confederation, then the United Colonies, in May 1643, as a 'perpetual league of friendship for offence and defence'. And he was a persistent and articulate voice, both encouraging colonists to keep friendships with Indian chiefs warm and trusting, whilst at the same time urging them to be vigilant for he (presciently) anticipated a general native uprising against the English.

Yet the last decade of his life was spent in London, separated by 3,000 miles from his second wife Susanna and his Plymouth family, and from his beautiful Careswell estate. He remained an ambassador for the Puritan colonies, sponsoring an Act of Parliament to establish the New England Corporation, tasked with converting Indians to Christianity in New England. He also clearly sympathised with the victorious Parliamentarians, though he was no party to the execution of Charles I. Cromwell evidently valued him and used his considerable diplomatic talents firstly as one of the seven members of the Committee for Compounding with Delinquents. It was a thankless task to deal with defeated and resentful Royalists but he alone of the Committee's members was retained for a second term, a reflection on his tact and sensitivity towards the disappointed. Cromwell employed him as member of a High Court convened to investigate a plot against his life in 1654; he also made him a member of the Arbitration Committee created to adjudicate on issues arising from the Anglo-Dutch War after its conclusion with the Treaty of Westminster. Finally, Cromwell appointed him in 1655 one of three commissioners accompanying the naval expedition to Hispaniola in the Caribbean, the aim of which was to establish a new English, and Protestant, colony on Spanish Catholic territory. By a curious circularity, his career had started and now ended with an expedition to plant a new colony, for he became ill with fever on Hispaniola that year and did not live to see the humiliating failure of the expedition.

Although his career in England is of some passing interest, Edward Winslow's true significance was in the New World; a son of Worcester had made an indelible mark on the other side of the Atlantic, where he was regarded (by his contemporary Cotton Mather) as a 'Hercules' who was 'from his very early days accustomed unto the crushing of that sort of serpents' (which delivered Massachusetts) 'from the designs of many troublesome adversaries that were petitioning unto the Parliament against them'. He was a founding father of the English settlement in America, he was a diplomat, a politician, and just as important, he was a sympathetic chronicler and interpreter of Indian culture and language.

Early Schooling at Worcester

From the fifteenth century in England there developed a growing demand for regular schooling, coinciding with the spread of literacy, and the exploitation of the printing press. Ambitious merchants and gentry sought an education which would equip their sons for a profession, or for an apprenticeship. The Tudor Age was therefore one in which a considerable number of new schools were founded, with most towns of even modest size boasting a new grammar school. This was partly a consequence of the redistribution of monastic resources in the Henrician Reformation, such as the King's School foundations (see Chapter 5), and also a result of private endowment, in which merchants established a local grammar school to meet the demand for literacy, book-keeping skills and more than that, a grounding in the classics. These schools therefore represented a new approach to learning, that of humanism, which focused both on the culture and language of the Ancient World, but which also emphasised the importance of the vernacular, so that in the words of one notable humanist, Juan Vives, schoolmasters would 'become custodians of the treasury of their language'.

Worcester had two grammar schools. There had been a medieval school from perhaps as early as the 7th century, catering for the relatives of monks and other children intending to join Worcester's Priory, and by the late Middle Ages it had come under the control of the city's guilds. It suffered when the King's School was founded, and at that point it had been declared unnecessary. However, the city council wanted it to be revived, and when it was refounded with a royal charter at the start of Elizabeth's reign, it was administered by local merchants, one of whom, Thomas Wylde, a wealthy clothier, gave land 'to Erect and stablish a Free School within the Cytie for ever to bringe up youth in there and other lernynge which shall make them mete and redie for the King's grammar School'. The school's master was 'to be a manne hole in bodye, honeste and virtuous and learned in good and cleyne latyn literature'. The refoundation of the Worcester Royal Grammar School well exemplifies several larger national themes, the interest of the commercial classes in providing a good education for local children, and the importance of inculcating a mastery of the classical languages.

The King's School rapidly established itself after its inauguration in 1541, and

Edward Winslow's headmaster, Henry Bright, won a national reputation as a schoolmaster, the famous antiquarian Anthony Wood recording in his *Fasti Oxonienses* that 'he had a most excellent facility in instructing youths in Latin and Greek and Hebrew, most of whom were afterwards sent to the universities'. In just the same way Thomas Fuller, in his *Worthies of England*, wrote that: 'for my part I behold this Master Bright placed by Divine Providence in this city, in the Marches, that he may communicate the Lustre of Grammar learning to youth in both England and Wales.' The school roll was large for a provincial school – some 150 boys at any one time, perhaps 90% of whom were sons of the county gentry. It reflected the esteem in which he came to be held in the county and beyond; it seems that the King's School became the county school, while the Elizabethan grammar school ministered more to the city itself. Some of Bright's boys came from as far afield as Cardigan and Caernarvonshire for, as Wood indicated, he was famed for his ability to place his pupils at Oxford and Cambridge. In his first decade as headmaster (1589-1599) thirty-six matriculated at the two universities, while 156 more matriculated in the remaining years before he died in office in 1627.

Winslow's father was a merchant, and he saw an education at the King's School, like many aspiring men of his class, as a means for his son to access a lucrative career in the Church or in the Law. Large numbers of those King's Scholars attending the Universities became churchmen, university and school teachers, or lawyers, like John Vaughan, who progressed from King's to Christ Church, Oxford, then Inner Temple, before becoming MP for Cardiganshire in 1629 and, according to Samuel Pepys, 'one of the greatest speakers in the House (of Commons)'.

If the core of Bright's curriculum was the trinity of Greek, Latin and Hebrew, beyond that he had a profound influence on pupils like Winslow because he introduced them to the work of leading Protestant thinkers. Henry Bright was himself an eloquent and magnetic preacher, reflecting his deep Reformed faith. He ensured that if Worcestershire itself harboured significant pockets of Catholicism, the Cathedral Close would be a model of Reformation orthodoxy, as prescribed by both Elizabeth I and James I. Winslow inherited his evangelism and like several others who had been taught by Bright (Thomas Brewer and William Fitzer, for example) he became a printer, and was apprenticed to a master specialising in Puritan works.

CHAPTER 10

Worcester and the First English Civil War

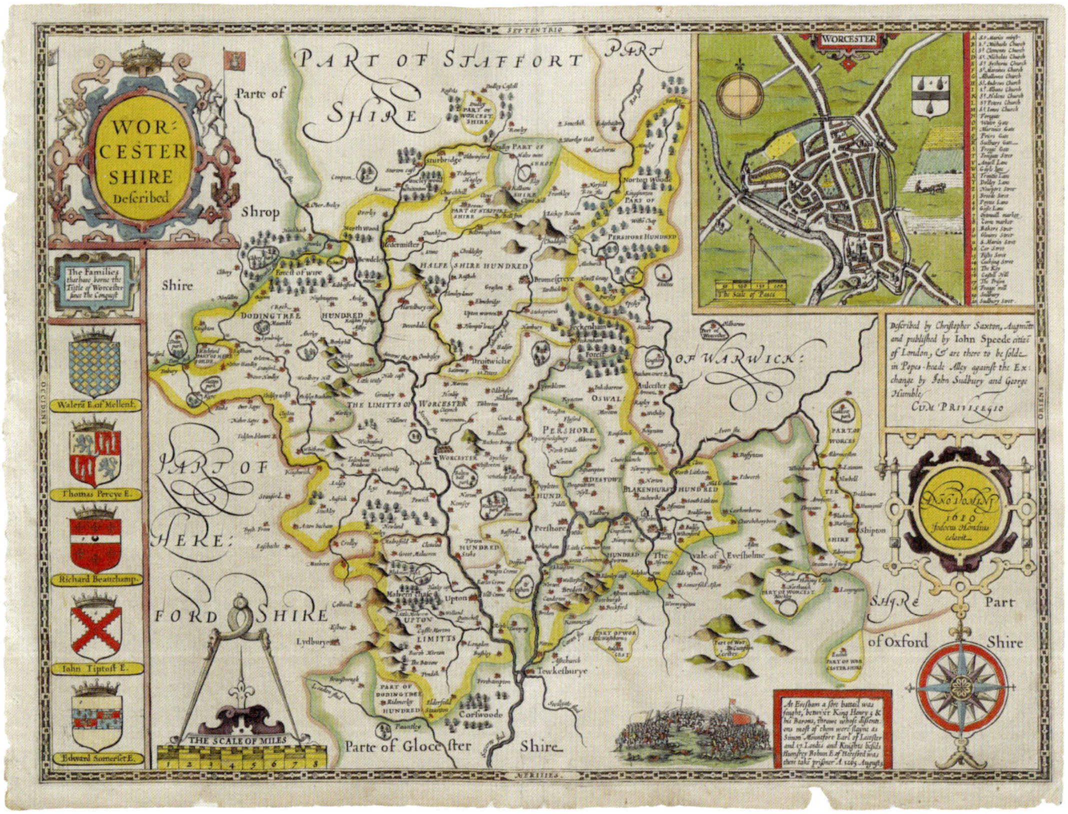

Speed's map of Worcestershire, 1611/12.

Events at Worcester book-end the story of the First Civil War in England from 1642 to 1646 which culminated in Charles I's defeat and capture. They helped generate a myth, that of the 'Faithful City'. They also indicated Worcester's continuing strategic importance, especially for the Royalist cause: it lay astride the King's supply route from Wales to Oxford and from Chester in the north to Bristol in the south-west and the contest for control of its bridging points over the Severn and the Teme (Powick, Upton-upon-Severn, Bewdley and Worcester itself) explains the repeated military clashes in the county between 1642 and 1646. Furthermore, Worcestershire was essential to arming the Crown: the city itself was a source of gunpowder, cannon came from Dudley's furnaces, shot from Stourbridge, and steel from the north of the county. In addition to all this there was an issue of sentiment: the King himself also came to believe Worcester to be markedly loyal and enthusiastic in his support.

Yet in reality it was not that simple; for the duration of the struggle, there was palpable tension in the city between Royalist and Parliamentary adherents. The merchant, clothier and yeomen classes in Worcester tended to sympathise with Parliament, their Puritan leanings being reflected in the city Council's vigorous objections in 1640 to the Laudian practices of Dean Mainwaring (his adoption of altar rails and a high altar). This perhaps explains the city's initial apathy towards published orders of the King's Commission of Array in July 1642, the Crown's attempt to recruit trained bands of men to fight in a future conflict. But by August Royalists in the city – traditional Anglicans and citizens who thought Parliament had exceeded its authority in challenging Charles and his ministers – were re-asserting themselves, and just as the King was raising his standard at Nottingham, Worcester was being dragged back into line by the surrounding county gentry, many of whom were devoted Cavaliers; loyalists like Sir Thomas Lyttleton of Frankley promised men and these county leaders set the tone, a total of 7,000 men being raised for the King in the first year of the war.

Still, the wild behaviour of some Cavaliers in the city in the early weeks of the war alienated many citizens, leading them to petition the Mayor about plundering marauders. The city's adherence to the crown was only secured by the arrival of a force of Royalist dragoons in mid-September, led by Sir John Byron. They were escorting treasure from Oxford bound for the King in Shrewsbury, the knowledge of which explains the close attention paid by the Parliamentary general, the Earl of Essex, who pursued Byron into the county with an army of 20,000 men.

Essex decided to implement several strategies. Firstly, to break into Worcester and secure it; secondly, to block off any retreat west of the city to Shrewsbury by Byron and his troopers. Worcester's first taste of action in a war which would continue to devastate families, households and property for the coming years, occurred on 22 September when Colonel John Brown led between 500 and 1000 Parliamentary troops in a ham-fisted assault on Worcester's weak and rotten southern defences, in particular the ill-defended Sudbury (Sidbury) Gate. A sharp cavalier counter-attack killed four or five assailants, and Brown and his men retreated to the west bank of the Severn at Upton-upon-Severn. Royalist confidence was further augmented by the arrival of Prince Rupert and his cavalry at Pitchcroft, west of the city.

They would be in action a day later, when Parliamentary forces moved on Worcester, prompted into action by false rumours that Byron was preparing to flee the city for

Worcestershire Archive and Archaeology Service

Medieval Powick Bridge, site of a key Civil War skirmish, 23 September 1642.

Shrewsbury. What would transpire, the skirmish at Powick, may not deserve the appellation 'battle,' but it was still significant, for nationally this was the first military engagement of the two rival armies in the Civil War, one which established Rupert's colourful reputation as one of the 'stars' of the war. Nehemiah Wharton, a sergeant in Denzil Holles's Parliamentary regiment, has left vivid testimony of what happened when his commanding officer, Colonel Sandys, led his soldiers up to the bridge over the Teme at Powick, heading for Worcester and aiming to interdict Byron's retreat. He starts by repeating the (erroneous) belief that:

> The treacherous inhabitants discovered Parliament's positions to the Prince (Rupert) and he forthwith set some troops to lye in ambush, who brake down a hedge and lay in the field on the right of them; the treacherous citizens attending them in multitudes with muskets who lay on each side of the hedge...
> (The battle was preceded by a truce). The

> Prince's forces went to intercept Sandys and his troops (near Powick). The Prince met them down a narrow lane. He asked them who they were for and Sandys answered, 'For King and Parliament.' He replied, 'Not for the king alone? And he (Sandys) answered, 'No.' Then said the Prince, 'For the King have at you,' and the Colonel answered, 'For the Parliament have at you.' And so they discharged at each other. The rest followed them and presently those in the ambush (down the lane) fired upon them and also the musketeers behind the hedges. The horsemen immediately fell to their swords so that for a space of almost an hour the skirmish was exceeding hot. I heard the Prince say that our men fought more like lions than men. The cavaleers (sic) boast wonderfully and swear most hellishly that the next time they meet us they will make but a mouthful of us, but I am persuaded the Lord has given us a small victory. For they left at their fright in the city some horses, trunks and other things all which His Excellency hath seized on.
>
> Colonel Essex is made governor of the city.

The larger picture was that the initial exchange on and around Powick Bridge severely damaged Rupert's cavalry, killing and wounding many Cavalier officers who were at the front of the clash of arms. On the other hand, the Parliamentary line broke and, in stampeding back down the lane and across the bridge, trampled and killed their own soldiers, some of whom drowned in the Teme when pushed off the bridge into the river. Parliamentary forces retreated to re-group at Upton. The Royalists claimed they killed about 80 enemy soldiers. But they did not stay on to consolidate their hold on Worcester; Rupert decided to use the breathing space to ensure Byron got his precious treasure to the King in Shrewsbury, and the Cavaliers vacated the city.

Valentine Green, the eighteenth-century historian of Worcester, strikingly describes the vindictiveness and ill-discipline of Essex and his men when they occupied the city, dwelling especially on the desecration and pillage of the Cathedral where 'every sort of vulgar abuse and wanton destruction was effected on the altar which was pulled down; vestments and furniture were destroyed', horses were stabled in the nave and the aisles were used as latrines. Stores and provisions were unearthed, some of them sent by the collegians of Oxford to sustain Royalist forces. Green goes on to recount Essex's punishment for citizens he believed had fortified the Cavaliers in the Powick battle. The Mayor, Edward Soley, and Alderman Green, who were deemed to be Royalist supporters, were arrested and sent under heavy guard to London. Gallows were erected in the marketplace for those found to be traitors; 220lb of plate was loaded onto a waggon and dispatched to Parliament in London, the city was fined £5,000 and forced to pay for the quartering and fuel of its occupying force. Fortunately for Worcester this hostile tide ebbed soon enough, for Parliamentary troops were forced to abandon the city, racing to intercept the King at Edgehill near Banbury in late October 1642, in a bid to stop him getting to London. By the end of the year the King held the county and the city entirely, even if pockets, like Evesham, remained sympathetic to his enemies.

For nearly four years Worcester survived intermittent blockade, and the county was criss-crossed by rival forces whose piratical raids on property brought about a growing exhaustion. By 1644, for example, war-weary Worcestershire was discussing a joint petition with Shropshire calling for peace from both sides in the conflict. It did not help that the Princes Maurice and Rupert billeted their troops in Worcester during much of 1644, with Prince Maurice appointed Lieutenant Colonel of Worcester; he and his retinue drained the city accounts by their demands for food and victuals. In fact, the woes faced by civilians, subject to violence and exaction, persisted until, by 1646, a decisive conclusion was in sight. Cromwell's New Model Army had won a definitive victory at Naseby in June 1645 and the following months saw Parliament mop up Royalist strongholds to apply an effective tourniquet on the last remaining pockets of resistance. Parliamentary forces in Evesham from the east, Gloucester in the south and Castle Frome to the west cut the city off from its supply lines in the autumn of 1645 but it defiantly continued to reinforce its defences, clearing the suburbs to improve the defenders' field of fire, which involved demolishing the church and hospital of St. Oswald in the north of the city.

By May 1646 Worcester's situation had grown seemingly impossible; the King had handed himself over to the Scots, Parliamentary sieges of Royalist strongholds in Worcestershire at Madresfield, Hartlebury and Dudley had ended with their surrender, and Worcester itself now faced a force of some 2,500 to 5,000 New Model Army troops, led by Colonel Whalley, encamped outside the city walls. He voiced a growing frustration in Parliamentary ranks at the city's stubbornness: 'Worcester,' he said, 'are now the only Troublers of the kingdom... And they deserve to be dealt with in an exemplary way, even to be made a prey to the soldiers.'

Indeed, Worcester was the last Royalist fastness in England to learn that on 10 June the King at Newcastle had ordered his garrison commanders 'upon honourable terms to quit those towns, castles and forts entrusted to you by us', hearing only weeks later unofficially from a copy of the declaration purchased from a news-stand. All the while Whalley completed the encirclement, occupying the suburb of St John's in the west from which to assail the bridge – and its fortified gate – over the Severn. Whalley's forces had to beat off a vigorous counter-attack here, made by 500 Royalist foot and 200 horse in a determined bid to dislodge the besiegers; *c.*100 Parliamentary soldiers were killed in a bloody clash on 12 June as some of those being blockaded by-passed Parliamentary battle-lines, penetrating the backs of suburban houses. Whalley continued to tighten the screw with the construction of a bridge of boats to cross the Severn to the north of the city, and slowly – as Parliament's hold strengthened – any sense of unity behind the city's defences began to evaporate. Henry Washington, the city's governor, clung on because of his loyalty to the King, for he had been ordered to hold the city; but also, because he and others had long and bitter memories of Parliamentary depredations the previous time their soldiers occupied the city in 1642.

Yet the behaviour of Washington's own troops, a majority of the 1,500 of whom were Irish, alienated many citizens. Progressive cuts in their pay as the siege dragged on made the soldiers more combustible, and explain the growing rate of desertion in late June, as does their knowledge that those taken under arms faced an automatic death sentence. 'A great disorder prevailed', writes Green, and in addition to that 'want of discipline', the city was suffering from severe shortages of provisions, and from the exhaustion of its ammunition. Henry Townshend of Elmley Lovett, who wrote a valuable diary of the whole civil war period in Worcestershire, describes how in July 1646, 'the city began to grow so mutinous that … they will throw the soldiers over the wall or club them…being now as all quiet people are weary of war, desiring their trading go on'. The arrival of Major-General Rainsborough to take over from Whalley concentrated collective minds, the bishop, 'a temperate moderator in discussion' (Green) hosting talks between Worcester's leaders at the bishop's palace. Even so it took weeks for the truce negotiated on 27 June with Whalley to evolve into final surrender on 19 July, as Washington held out for better terms.

Rainsborough presided over that surrender: the garrison was to be disbanded, its men promising not to take up arms again, all arms and ammunition were to be handed over and for his part Rainsborough agreed that his men would not loot the city. After a service in the Cathedral on 23 July, the garrison marched out and up Rainbow Hill in the north-east of the city, where a formal ceremony of surrender was held. The general (now appointed Worcester's governor) secured Worcester's future loyalty to Parliament by fining Royalist delinquents, bringing back onto the city Council councillors who had been exiled for their loyalty to the Parliamentary cause, and by systematically reducing the city's fortifications, hoping to ensure that Worcester could not be a threat if it should backslide into the Royalist cause in the future.

Worcester was the last major centre to hold out for the King in the First Civil War; only Wallingford Castle stood firm for longer in England. Yet, while there would be no further military engagement during Charles I's lifetime, his execution in 1649 and his son's fierce determination to avenge him would ensure that Worcester would yet again be prominent in the story of the English Civil Wars (see next chapter).

CHAPTER 11

The Battle of Worcester 1651

Of all Worcester's historic events none is better known than the Battle of Worcester of 3 September 1651. King Charles II's campaign to avenge his father's death and regain the English throne ended in humiliation and crushing defeat in Worcester at the hands of Oliver Cromwell and the New Model Army. A third Civil War was over before it had barely started; hopes of a Royalist triumph of arms were finally dashed. Charles's Scottish allies were subsequently mercilessly hunted down, many of his English supporters imprisoned, exiled or executed, and for the king himself Worcester would be just the first act of a long and perilous flight to France in which his ingenuity, derring-do and sheer luck would provide plentiful copy for future Royalist myth-makers. For Cromwell, victory at Worcester would be proof of Divine approbation, 'a marvellous salvation', and a 'crowning mercy'; had Charles II prevailed the very existence of the Commonwealth, the Republic Cromwell had worked to create, would have been threatened. It would prove to be Cromwell's final battle; he had never lost a military engagement, a tribute to his own courageous example at the head of his troops, to his strategic and tactical brilliance, and to his extraordinary spiritual force, an amalgam of self-belief and strong faith in the cause.

The execution of Charles I in January 1649 drove his young son across the North Sea from Continental exile to put himself in the hands of Scots whose opposition to his father's religious policy had provoked the First Civil War. Now, their disapproval of the regicides, and disappointment with their erstwhile Parliamentary allies, inclined Scottish leaders to join Charles. From the outset, though, Charles's rebel army was divided between English Cavaliers, many of whom were long-standing loyalists, and Scottish Presbyterians of a very different ilk. Worse, his forces were greatly reduced when Cromwell and his experienced New Model soldiers forced-marched north to surprise and beat the Royalists at Dunbar. And when the able young Major-General John Lambert then routed the Scots at Inverkeithing, Charles now faced a choice of either retreating (to the Highlands or back to France) or advancing into England, with the aim of prompting a popular uprising in London.

Cromwell, convinced long supply lines would undermine it, ushered the Royalist army south – to the consternation of a nervous Council of State in London, fearful of the consequences for regicides of a royal restoration. But he prepared his ground meticulously, denying Charles's army the ability to recruit or re-supply as it marched further into England, harrying Royalists like the Earl of Derby at Wigan, whilst at the same time mobilising militias from southern and midlands counties in

The Picture Art Collection / Alamy Stock Photo

Oliver Cromwell surveys troops before Worcester, 1651.

readiness for action. By the time Charles reached the West Midlands he had only *c.*10,000 Scots and perhaps 2,000 English soldiers, and his army had the regrettable appearance of a foreign invading force, one which was compounded in the battle itself when the King fought under a Scottish standard, 'proud Scotland's royal shield'. On one hand the Scots' reputation for ill-discipline and looting repelled many would-be volunteers, and on the other hand, many English were simply war-weary. By contrast, Cromwell's army of 30,000, comprising militia and regular New Model troops, was well organised, well fed and supplied, and was battle-hardened.

Charles's troops were herded away from London towards the west by Cromwell's pursuing companies; for a time, it seemed Oxford, Charles I's loyal capital in the First Civil War, might be the goal, but the young king determined on Worcester, the 'Faithful City', the last defiant stronghold of Royalist resistance in the siege of 1646. Its proximity to Wales, a rich Royalist recruiting ground; its agricultural wealth (to feed his army) and its ironworking (to forge his army's weaponry); its strategic position, guarding a crossing of the Severn; and finally, the legend of its Cavalier enthusiasm – all persuaded him to decide on Worcester as his base. He was to be rudely disabused about the city's Royalist fervour. Whilst it is true that the city decided not to resist the invading army, and that the mayor and corporation subsequently welcomed the King with all due ceremony, the fact is that having suffered a prolonged siege five years earlier, local leaders made a strictly pragmatic decision to avoid bloodshed and follow the path of least resistance. A more accurate indication of sentiment was the reaction of townsmen to King Charles's personal appeal made on Pitchcroft, the open space to the west of the city. There he issued a summons to all able-bodied men in the county from sixteen to sixty to assemble with horses and weapons and arms. Even 'well-affected gentry' chose to stay at home; the generality of men ignored the muster. Of those who responded, a significant number were Catholic, perpetuating that strain of Worcestershire loyalism from the start of the First Civil War.

To the consternation of many citizens the King's's army settled comfortably into life in Worcester, with Charles hoping to use the city as a rallying point for Royalists in the West Country. Troops were billeted inside the city walls in private houses, the overspill camping outside on Pitchcroft to the west and to the south by the Severn crossing at Upton-upon Severn. Provisioning so many men and their camp-followers severely tested local resources and the citizens were compelled to pay for the army's food and drink.

Troops were set to work to rebuild the walls – in a poor state of repair – and to construct a new Fort Royal outside the walls to the south-east of the city, creating a star-shaped bastion – an artillery platform – to protect Worcester from attacks from London and the east. The necessity of looking to Worcester's defences was made the more urgent by the arrival in the Vale of Evesham on 27 August of some 30,000 troops led by Cromwell himself who made Spetchley his headquarters, but a few miles from Fort Royal. These soldiers – and their women, who acted as nurses to the injured – were a huge burden on the villages and farms of the Vale.

Cromwell's army had the benefit of more – and more powerful – artillery pieces than those of the Scots. Outnumbering his opponent, Cromwell planned first to prevent Charles reaching London, Wales or the West Country, and then to surround the Royalist army in Worcester before annihilating it. He was completely successful in this strategic aim. He dispatched troops north to Bewdley to block any Royalist escape to Wales; further afield Gloucester, Hereford, Ludlow and Bristol were fortified for Parliament to repel any Scottish break-out from Worcester. And to the south and west of the city just before the battle (on 28 August) he seized the initiative from a criminally negligent Royalist general, Edward Massey, who left the key Severn crossing-point at Upton-upon-Severn badly undermanned. Malcolm

Atkin, the battle's historian, concludes that Massey's dereliction 'was to prove fatal to the whole course of the battle'. For a surprise attack there led by Major-General Lambert snatched Upton's bridge, enabling Parliamentary forces to pour across and start to secure the area to the west of the city. Now Cromwell, moving the rest of his army up to the high ground east of Worcester above Fort Royal, could attack from west and east of the city. He made the first move of the battle on 3 September, sending General Fleetwood and his troops already on the west bank of the Severn to attack the Scots, who were encamped on the flood plain across the River Teme above Powick, a village to the south-west of the city. Powick bridge had been partly demolished by the Royalists, and the crossing was desperately defended by Scots occupying the church tower and nearby mill; a Parliamentary eyewitness described the fighting as 'very hot…till we had beaten them out of the ground'. Charles II's personal intervention at Powick that morning to try to stiffen Royalist resistance was unavailing, and he retreated back to the Cathedral tower, whence he could watch the unfolding battle.

Another crossing of the Severn, east of Powick bridge, to enable the two Parliamentary armies easily to link up south of Worcester, necessitated the construction of a bridge of boats. Tenacious Scottish defence of the meadowland north of this makeshift traverse pinned down Parliamentary troops until Cromwell himself, leading brigades of experienced cavalry men, which included his own Lifeguards, swept in from the east to provide new momentum. He is said to have been the first to charge across the bridge, helping establish a bridgehead and setting his troops on their way north to the city, before he returned to Red Hill. Desperate hand-to-hand fighting succeeded in clearing the Scots from their path. In Cromwell's report of the battle to the Speaker of the House of Commons he wrote: 'We beat the enemy from hedge to hedge, till we beat them into Worcester.' Success to the west of the city culminated in Fleetwood's men eventually driving the Scots through the parish of St John's and – in the eighteenth-century account of Valentine Green – 'routing them and killing many and pursuing the rest to the drawbridge and gate of the city'.

Cromwell yet had to deal with the bulk of the Scottish army assembled around Sudbury (now Sidbury) Gate below Fort Royal, opposite his own forces south-east of the city, which were drawn up on Red Hill and Perry Hill. Observing the reverses his brigades suffered around Powick, the king determined on a bold move to turn the course of the battle, leading a column of men to charge up Red Hill, whilst Royalist cavalry under the Duke of Hamilton charged out of St Martin's Gate in the east of the city to attack Parliamentary gun emplacements on adjacent Perry Hill. There was initial success with Hamilton's Scots capturing the Perry Hill cannon, and – as Cromwell averred – the Royalists 'made a very considerable fight with us,

Courtesy of the Council of the National Army Museum

The Battle of Worcester, 3 September 1651. Troops approach the bridge over the Severn, with the city in the background.

for three hours space, but in the end, we beat them totally, and pursued him up to his Royal Fort, which we took…(and) we turned his own guns upon him.' All Charles's own flamboyant bravery, riding in the thick of the action, could not arrest the flight of his cavalry; he himself just made it through Sudbury Gate, such was the press of fleeing soldiers. Barely stopping to collect personal effects, Charles escaped through the city's north gate, and fled on the road to Ombersley.

Once Cromwell's troops had pushed through Sudbury Gate and into the city the battle continued, with the king's cavalry men ferociously resisting street by street until being eventually outnumbered and forced to surrender. An account by a Scottish officer, later imprisoned, describes how the Parliamentary soldiers 'fell to plunder and made great slaughter of the enemy, by reason of their greediness after pillage', while the contemporary news-sheet, *Mercurius Politicus*, recorded that Worcester had 'indeed become a sad spectacle, and was very noisome by reason of the multitude of dead carcasses both of man and beast, for the fight was very fierce and the slaughter of the enemy great'. John Aubrey, the seventeenth-century diarist and biographer, salaciously chronicled curious instances of angel lust among the corpses, for 'the penes of the dead stripped bodies for two or three days were erect', a frequent consequence for men dying a violent death. Some of these cadavers littered the cloisters and the cathedral itself, which served as a cage for hundreds of Scottish prisoners under guard. So fetid was the air that Parliament afterwards gave a grant for cleaning and purifying the building.

A battle which had cost anything between 2,000 and 4,000 Scottish lives, as opposed to between 100 and 200 Parliamentarians, was a stunning victory for Cromwell but he recognised that although 'this hath been a very glorious mercy', the battle had been far from easy – indeed, it was 'as stiff a contest for four or five hours as ever I have seen'. He was certainly not content to leave it at that. Plans had been laid even before the conflict to net the king should he flee, and to mop up Royalist survivors. Worcester itself would bear witness to Parliament's ruthlessness, a reflection of its distrust of a city which had welcomed and hosted a Royal rebel. The city's wealth was considered the rightful perquisite of the conquerors. It was said that 'all houses (were) ransacked from top to bottom', loyal Parliamentary supporters suffering equally in the indiscriminate sack. Those found to have sided with the king faced imprisonment, heavy fines, or the confiscation of estates. And a city which had already lost housing stock in the siege of 1646 had suffered yet again as houses were demolished both in preparation for the battle and in its violent aftermath.

While Worcester collectively licked its wounds, attention shifted to the hunt for the royal quarry as Charles endured scrapes and near misses to make his way up to Shropshire, where he hid at White Ladies and Boscobel, before a six-week adventure which took him south via Bristol, Amesbury and Hambledon to eventual escape by boat from Shoreham harbour, bound for Fécamp in France. Charles's survival perpetuated life in the Royalist cause and paved the way for a future Restoration. He never returned to Worcester – he had sensed the 'Faithful City' was too ambivalent, and its support in 1651 half-hearted.

Although Cromwell's victory was complete and durable in terms of his own lifetime, the long-term prospects for the Commonwealth remained uncertain. The valedictory oration of Hugh Peters, the Parliamentary army chaplain, given when addressing the victorious troops at Worcester, proved premature: 'When their wives and children should ask them where they had been and what news,' he declaimed, channelling Shakespeare's *Henry V*, 'they should say they had been at Worcester, where England's sorrows began, and where they were happily ended'. The Restoration of Charles II in 1660 re-opened old wounds and proved for some anything but a happy ending.

CHAPTER 12

Worcester and James II

The first decade of Charles II's reign (1660-1685) was conspicuous for a remarkable cultural and intellectual flowering, but its last half was overshadowed by the issue of the succession. Despite his energetic love life, the king had been unable to father a legitimate heir and by 1675 it was clear that his successor would be his brother James, Duke of York, an open and avowed Catholic. The prospect awakened deep and dark fears in a national psyche moulded by historic Catholic conspiracies. These had sought to overthrow English Protestant liberties: the spectres of the Spanish Armada, the Gunpowder Plot, the Irish rebellion of 1641, and of imported Irish soldiery, which Worcester experienced in 1646 and 1651, materialised with every popular spasm of anti-Popery. It did not help that just across the Channel Louis XIV of France provided a vivid contemporary illustration of how a monarch could rule absolutely (without a parliament) and could destroy a Protestant church; in 1685 he revoked the Edict of Nantes and expelled the Protestant (Huguenot) community from France. Louis, Charles II and James were close friends and allies. Fears for a future with James as monarch, perhaps emulating Louis, explain the unsuccessful but vicious battle the Whig opposition fought to exclude him from the succession in the late 1670s.

Worcester made its own – distinctive – contribution to James's troubled reign (1685-88) which culminated in the Glorious Revolution at the end of 1688. At the start, along with the rest of the country, it gave the new king the benefit of the doubt, the city proclaiming him in February 1685, 'with all usual Ceremonys of Drums, trumpets and the City band and Musick with Bells Ringing and Bonfires with great Acclamations of Joye'.

That summer James's troops crushed the West Country rebellion of Charles's illegitimate son, the Duke of Monmouth, while the rest of the country, including Worcester, remained loyal. Within months the national mood darkened, as it became apparent that James was not content to consider his Catholic faith simply to be a personal matter but – rather – was bent on implementing a programme to establish for English Catholics the same political and religious freedoms enjoyed by Anglicans. What made him the more dangerous was his deeply authoritarian streak; he had been an admiral in the navy and retained all his life a tendency to martial despotism.

He would demonstrate both an arrogant disregard for constitutional law and an indifference to Anglican susceptibilities. A believer in the Divine Right of Kings, he assumed powers to dispense with the Test Act of 1673, legislation which had effectively ensured all office-holders were Anglicans. He used these prerogative functions to appoint Catholics to the army, prompting concerns that a tame military might eventually enforce a Catholic settlement on the country. He published two Declarations of Indulgence, extending toleration to Catholics and Dissenters. By 1688 he was purging local councils and pressurising MPs to try and manufacture a Parliament which would do his will, that is – repeal the Test Acts and enshrine in law the equal status of Catholics and Dissenters. At the same time, he started to bully Anglican bishops – and through them the clergy – to prohibit any preaching against royal religious policy. He also commenced an assault on the universities of Oxford and Cambridge, attempting to break the Anglican monopoly there. Meanwhile, the opening of a Catholic chapel in Lime Street in London was to be a precedent for other chapels like it beyond the capital.

One such chapel appeared in Worcester in the Tything. When James II visited the city in 1687 he not only processed from the gate to the Bishop's Palace along a way strewn with flowers and covered by white Worcester broadcloth, and toured the sights of the city including Fort Royal, the battle grounds of 1642 and 1651 and the cathedral, but he also then 'proceeded', according to Valentine Green, 'in solemnity, to a popish chapel on the east side of Foregate Street, built at his accession to the throne'. The chapel had only just opened in 1685, built by local Catholics, emboldened by the sea-change in religious policy allowing open Catholic worship, something James himself had initiated. 'On arrival at the chapel His Majesty asked if they (the accompanying Mayor and aldermen) would not go in?' 'The Mayor, Thomas Shewring, with becoming firmness replied, 'I think we have attended Your Majesty too far already.' 'Depositing the sword before the King in the chapel, and making their reverence to him, they retired and returned to divine service in the Cathedral', although an alternative version has it that, with rather less decorum, they repaired to *The Green Dragon* and drank ale until the monarch's mass was over. The King was making a point of overtly worshipping in a Catholic chapel in the lee of one of the principal Anglican cathedrals; it was a calculated provocation. As was his insistence – at dinner in the Palace the same evening - that his Romish chaplain, rather than the Bishop himself, should say grace. The determined resistance of Worcester's Mayor and aldermen typifies the defiant attitude of many Protestant office-holders nationally, as relations deteriorated between King and Protestant subjects.

The King's controversial attempt to intimidate the two ancient universities found a prebendary (and later Bishop) of Worcester, John Hough (1651-1743), at its heart. The occasion – the election of the President of Magdalen College, Oxford in April 1687 – became a *cause célèbre*, for the death of the incumbent, Dr Henry Clarke, prompted James II to command the Fellows to elect one Anthony Farmer as its President, a Catholic and a man the Fellows claimed to be 'debauched and lewd'. The King saw this appointment as a golden opportunity to break the Anglican monopoly at Oxford. The Fellows

Memorial to Bishop John Hough, Worcester Cathedral, 1743.

claimed that Farmer was statutorily ineligible and that, in any case, he had paid someone to procure a naked woman for him; and that the arrival of the King's letter to the Fellows had coincided with Farmer appearing drunk in an Abingdon public house, where he had caused consternation by trying to French kiss a young woman at the bar. They refused to comply with the King's wishes; instead, John Hough, an unobtrusive and unobjectionable Fellow of the College, was sworn in as the new President.

James II then changed tack; he now insisted they elect the Bishop of Oxford rather than the discredited Farmer, in Hough's place. They refused, provoking an incandescent King to travel down to Magdalen himself to settle the matter in September 1687. Once there he berated the assembled Fellows. To their argument that the College's oaths and statutes would not allow them to overthrow Hough for a royal nominee, he exploded, severely scolding them:

> Is this your Church of England's loyalty? Get ye gone. Know that I am your King and I command you to be gone, Go and admit the Bishop of Oxford head, Principal (whatever ye call it of your College). Let him know that refuses it – look to it. They shall find the weight of the sovereign's displeasure.

He ordered them to the College Chapel, but– despite the threat that 'they should expect to feel the heavy hand of an angry King' – they still refused to ditch Hough for the Bishop of Oxford. So, James sent his special commissioners to Oxford the following month, at which point Hough and the Fellows were cited to appear before them in the hall of Magdalen College. Hough was first to be summoned; when he refused to resign his claim, his name was ordered to be struck from the College books, and the Fellows commanded no longer to submit to him. Two subsequent appearances before the commissioners failed to induce him to abandon the Presidency. On the last occasion, after he had delivered a formal protest and vowed to appeal to the King in his courts of justice, one of the commissioners – Sir Thomas Jenner – demanded of him, 'Do you mean to huff us, sir?' and denied him his right to appeal. Hough continued to defy the King and his commissioners; when the Bishop of Oxford was admitted by proxy, Hough declined to hand over the keys of the President's lodgings, which were broken open by force. On 10 December the ecclesiastical commissioners declared Hough and the Fellows to be stripped of any ecclesiastical dignity on account of 'their contemptuous and disobedient behaviour'.

All James's haughty arrogance is evident in his bullying of the Fellows. Although he had temporarily got his way, the Magdalen College affair did much to convince observers that there was a sinister agenda to force England to submit to Catholic absolutism. Only in September 1688 did he relent, to order the reinstatement of Hough and the Fellows of Magdalen. By this time, James was facing foreign invasion from Dutch forces, invited in by representatives of the governing classes, and was hoping to win back support by a quick *volte-face*. It would prove to be a concession too late to stem the momentum moving towards revolutionary change. John Hough was later to be rewarded for his steadfastness by William of Orange's new regime, firstly with the bishopric of Oxford and then, in 1717, with that of Worcester, where he was a quiet but generous incumbent, dying there in 1743; he was buried in Worcester Cathedral.

This Glorious Revolution of 1688 saw another son of Worcester, John Somers (1651-1716), at the centre of events. Born in Claines, just to the north of Worcester, he was educated at the King's School and then at Trinity, Oxford, before being called to the bar at Middle Temple. There his intellectual brilliance won for him a golden reputation among Whig critics of the King. His politics chimed with theirs, for it is alleged he penned the *Just and Modest Vindication of the two Last Parliaments* in 1681, an eloquent apology for parliamentary government faced with a tyrannical monarch. By 1688 his stock had risen to the point that he was chosen as junior counsel for the defence of the Seven Bishops in a trial of enormous political importance. The bishops had been ordered by the Crown to instruct their clergy to read the Second Declaration of Indulgence from the pulpit on successive Sundays. If they did so they would be acquiescing in James's religious policy, and one implemented by prerogative not by statute law. Seven bishops, led by Archbishop Sancroft, petitioned the King to be excused from distributing and reading the Declaration; they made it clear that they believed the suspending power on which the Declaration was based to be illegal. The petition was subsequently published – evidently, not by the bishops themselves. Their defiance was unexpected and a shattering blow, and – unwisely – as he lashed out, James had them arrested for seditious libel.

At issue here were royal prerogative powers. Therefore, the trial assumed totemic significance for the opposition. The great historian, Thomas Macaulay, summarised the dramatic, clinching defence speech:

> Somers rose last. He spoke little more than five minutes; but every word was full of weighty matter; and when he sat down his reputation as an orator and a constitutional lawyer was established. He said: 'The Bishops could have no design to diminish the prerogative, because the king hath no prerogative. Seditious the petition could not be for the matter was strictly true. Malicious? – there could be nothing of malice for the occasion, instead of being sought, was forced on them. A libel it could not be, for the intent of the defendants was innocent and they kept strictly within the bounds of the law'.

Even intense royal pressure on the judges could not prevent their own discomfort about the prosecution case from communicating itself to the jury, which duly acquitted the defendants.

Judgement in the Bishops' trial coincided with the shocking news that James II's second wife, Mary of Modena, had given birth to a male heir. Now it seemed a Catholic royal line would be established in England; the succession would not pass, as many had consoled themselves, to his Protestant daughters from his first marriage, Mary and Anne. These events in late summer

1688, compounded by the build-up of James's army on Hounslow Heath, terrified conspiracy theorists who conjured a nightmare vision of a permanent Catholic despotism in England. The very day of the 'not guilty' verdict in the Bishops' trial, six peers and the suspended Bishop of London issued an invitation to William of Orange to bring a force to England against James.

John Somers took a leading part in the secret councils of those who planned the Glorious Revolution. And once William had landed in Torbay, marched to London, and put James to flight at the end of 1688, Somers was a key figure in framing a constitutional settlement which could make sense both of the vacuum created by that flight and the promotion of joint monarchs in place of James II. Elected as MP for Worcester in the Convention Parliament (1689), which was summoned to give statutory approval of the Revolution, Somers used his maiden speech to argue that James had forfeited his claim to the allegiance of the English people by his alliance with Louis XIV and with the Pope. It was Somers who won the day – against opponents in the Lords – in contending that the King had abdicated, leaving a vacant throne. 'He subverted the constitution, so breaking the original contract between the King and the people, and by violating the fundamental laws, and by avowing to govern by despotic powers'. Here is Somers, the articulate mouthpiece, and the incisive thinker, justifying a Revolution.

It comes as no surprise that Somers should then have been central to the drawing up of the Bill of Rights. Or that he should have found the words to convey to the general public just how significant was this revolution. In his *Vindication of the Proceedings of the Late Parliament of England* (1690) he boasted:

> The (late) proceedings were so fair, so prudent, so necessary and so advantageous to the nation and in particular the Church of England that all true Englishmen must needs acknowledge they owe to their representatives their privileges, their lives, their religion, their present and future security.

For Somers the supremacy of law was all: 'Our kings can never be arbitrary, absolute or tyrants'.

William III recognised Somers' importance: not only was he able both to understand and explain the revolution, but he was also a fierce defender of the legitimacy of a new King and Queen who ruled at the behest of Parliament. Somers became William's confidential advisor, rising from Solicitor-General to Attorney-General and then finally in 1697 to Lord Chancellor, as Baron Somers of Evesham. Although his last years saw him the victim of vicious Court intrigue, and he survived attempts to impeach him, he died in 1716 secure in the knowledge that the causes for which he had argued so passionately –the Established Church, Parliamentary ascendancy and the defeat of absolutism – had been irrevocably secured. His legacy lived on long after his death, especially in the New World. Thomas Jefferson, one of America's founding fathers, retained copies of Somers' books in his Library, and the American Bill of Rights is firmly based on Somers' 1689 Bill of Rights.

The Modern Age

Royal Worcester porcelain. One of the city's most famous products, in this case depicting the city itself, 1751.

Worcester in the centuries after the Glorious Revolution was characterised both by the strong sense of continuity with its medieval past and by dramatic changes brought about by the onset of a national industrial revolution. The Cathedral, at the centre of an extensive diocese, remained an important influence in the national Church but was also of consequence as local employer, as consumer and as a centre for music in the Anglican tradition; triennially it hosted the country's longest-running choral festival, the Three Choirs Festival, while it inspired the young Elgar to write and compose. Worcester was still an important market and craft centre for the region, and its ancient charter ensured it sent two burgesses to Parliament up to 1885. In that sense the zeal for parliamentary reform which seized neighbouring Birmingham in 1832 largely evaded long-time Tory Worcester which was already well-represented. In fact, Worcester is significant not for an excess of democratic enthusiasm, as was Birmingham, but because it came to typify the small borough corruption which disfigured parts of national politics until 1914.

The River Severn and the uneven – sometimes barely passable – road network converging on the city continued in the eighteenth century to make of Worcester a small inland port and transport hub. But nigh on a century of internal peace in Britain, combined with readier access to capital and a generation of inventors and entrepreneurs, produced benign conditions for two nation-wide revolutions which would profoundly affect Worcester's fortunes – those transforming transport and industry. The Worcester and Birmingham Canal enriched the city, which commanded the junction of the new canal with the River Severn. Birmingham's manufactured goods and raw materials such as coal had found a new outlet, passing through Worcester and thence travelling down to Bristol. Industry colonised the canal basins at Diglis and Lowesmoor. Where once high-quality cloth had defined Worcester's economy, the city became a world leader in glove, porcelain, vinegar and sauce production. The declining fortunes of most of these industries since the First World War typify a wider national retreat from manufacturing in the twentieth century.

If the nineteenth and early twentieth centuries were the country's democratic years, as large numbers successfully campaigned for the right to vote, the past one hundred years have been stained by successive wars, and Worcester has its own distinctive story to tell: of a critical contribution in 1914 at Gheluvelt to the preservation of the Allies' line at Ypres, and as a vital back-stop in the event of invasion in 1939/40.

CHAPTER 13
A Canal Transforms Worcester

Image produced by kind permission of Tudor House Museum from its Changing Face of Worcester collection- www.cfow.org.uk

Trows plying the River Severn at Worcester, with North Quay and Worcester Bridge in the background.

For centuries Worcester benefited economically from its position on the River Severn; trows – the indigenous Severn cargo boats – embarked from the quay-side on the river below the Cathedral, carrying commodities up to Shropshire and down to Bristol. Craftsmen had settled and then traded in Worcester's market-place for many years; as we have seen, the city developed a famous broadcloth industry which flourished in the sixteenth century. Then in the eighteenth century came the step-change described in the Introduction. Canals initiated the nation's transport revolution and enabled heavy goods to be hauled smoothly across the country, at a time when many roads were dangerous and sometimes impassable in winter. The financial pain, and the protracted period of construction, of the new Worcester and

Birmingham Canal would in time bring Worcester rich dividends, opening trade via Birmingham right up to Manchester, and enabling goods from the Midlands and the North, passing through Worcester, to travel on to Gloucester, Bristol and the West Country. This trade in heavy goods would bring with it new industries, and prompt the development of the city's two significant canal basins. By the middle of the nineteenth century, then, Worcester had become an important manufacturing city, a situation consolidated by the arrival of a rail link from 1851.

Since at least 1784 a canal to Birmingham had been regularly mooted by businessmen in Worcester to connect the collieries west of Birmingham to the Severn at Diglis. Coal was a vital fuel for many industrial processes, especially with the advent of steam power; it was also much in demand for domestic consumption. If the original impetus came from Worcester, then it is also true that Birmingham stood to gain enormously from a reliable link to the Severn. When opposition by some landowners and vested interests were overcome, and a parliamentary bill establishing the Worcester and Birmingham canal was passed in 1791, a song published in a Birmingham newspaper articulated the canal's potential for Birmingham's metal-manufacturers:

In Europe's grand Toy-shop how pleasing 'twill be
Well freighted the trows and the barges to see,
The country 'twill charm and new life give to trade,
When the seat of the Arts shall a sea-port be made.

However, it took 24 years for that vision to be realised, while the company faced recurring financial difficulties. This was a period of rapid inflation; more than this, all the time the canal was being constructed the country was engaged in mortal struggle with Revolutionary France. And although James Brindley, the first great canal engineer in the North and the Midlands, had generally followed water-courses when he laid out his canals, this new enterprise had to traverse hills and valleys, necessitating the digging of tunnels, cuttings and the construction of embankments and aqueducts. Inevitably it took longer, and cost much more, than originally envisaged. Worcester for long waited impatiently for the benefits of considerable investment to show. For the canal opened in stages from the Birmingham Gas Street Basin and its Worcester Wharf, creeping slowly towards Worcester and the Severn. The first few miles – the long summit level – were free of locks, but involved laborious digging out of several tunnels, the most famous being that at West Hill, King's Norton. As *Aris's Gazette* (the popular Birmingham publication) boasted when the tunnel opened: 'It extends 1½ miles and dead straight that it may be seen one end to the other and the quality of brickwork is well worthy of attention.' Millions of bricks were needed to line the tunnels, and for bridges and – further down the canal – for the locks. Brickworks were created all along the canal cutting, which were able to take advantage of the local Keuper marl, a good clay to be shaped and fired for bricks.

As each stage of the canal was completed, junketing and celebrations reflected the enthusiasm of locals who would benefit from fresh job opportunities and from cheaper fuel and more varied foodstuffs. At Selly Oak in 1797, for example, only 4 miles from the Gas Street Basin, *Berrow's Journal* reported that the canal's arrival and the landing of the first coal from Birmingham was celebrated with roasted ox and copious ale. Very quickly coal merchants hired wharfs and warehouses, and farmers used coal barges to carry grain back to Birmingham. This was well illustrated when in 1807 the cut reached Tardebigge Old Wharf, just under half way to Worcester. Merchants confidently increased the volume of traffic south from Birmingham and the tonnages of coal to supply the North Worcestershire countryside multiplied; meanwhile, independent carriers developed a return trade in timber and in wheat, barley and oats to feed the burgeoning town of Birmingham. These signs of success heartened the company's directors, many of whom could be forgiven for wondering whether the canal would ever get to Worcester; it had been 13 years since 'navvies' (navigators) dug the first sods of the cut south of Gas Street Basin and there were still 15 miles to go to reach the Severn. A board meeting at the Hop Pole Inn in Worcester in May 1811 determined to complete the canal project, agreeing to the construction of more than 50 locks in the process.

Martin Bache / Alamy Stock Photo

Section of the Tardebigge locks on the Worcester and Birmingham Canal, the longest flight of locks in the UK.

In fact, Tardebigge posed some of the most challenging demands on canal engineers anywhere in the country, for a steep descent of over 300 feet had to be negotiated to take the canal down to Stoke Prior and Hanbury, before the last push to Worcester. The hill at Tardebigge had first to be blasted and a tunnel over 500 yards long then excavated. On the south side a New Wharf was created; and thereafter a series of 30 locks for the drop down to Stoke Prior. This Tardebigge Flight is the longest run of locks in the country, and the Top Lock – 12 feet deep – is the deepest in England. Remarkably, this last stretch of the canal took much less time than had the first stage to Tardebigge. By 1815 the canal had reached Worcester, a basin being excavated at Lowesmoor, and a mile or so further on a second and larger basin being constructed at Diglis on the Severn.

Just as important was a set of negotiations back in Birmingham with the Birmingham Canal Company. Up to 1815 the Worcester Bar, as it was known, separated the wharves of the two canal companies in Gas Street Basin, those of the Worcester/Birmingham Canal and the Birmingham Canal. Across that 7-foot-wide bar goods had to be manually transferred from barge to barge; now an agreement was reached to create a lock in the bar to allow barges to move through from one to the other. Along with an existing agreement with the Stratford and Birmingham Canal, a whole new inter-linked navigable system was created. As the *Worcester Herald* boasted in December 1815: 'A direct water communication is thus opened from the North of England to Bristol and other parts of the West, with important consequences for the commerce of divers towns within its reach.'

With a neat sense of timing the 30-mile operation was completed and opened in December 1815, just after the Battle of Waterloo had summarily concluded the war. The canal was now set to transform Worcester's business and commercial fortunes. The very first barge arriving there on the day of the canal's opening that December illustrated its huge commercial potential; Thomas and Matthew Pickford, who ran a comprehensive carriers' firm with 116 boats and 400 horses, delivered a cargo of goods from Tardebigge, and promptly set out for a return journey travelling all the way up to Manchester with agricultural produce from the West. Within months heavy barges, laden with bricks, coal, grain and machinery, lime, limestone, salt, gravel, sand-ashes and manure would be tied up at Diglis Quay alongside fly-boats destined to make express deliveries to the North of England and back. The *Severn and Canal Carrying Co.* typifies the versatile nature of water-borne trade from the 1870s up to the advent of road traffic in the 1920s. Steam driven tugs guided narrow-boats laden with timber, wheat, sugar, cocoa and chocolate crumb up the Severn before horses took over at Diglis to pull the boats up the canal to Birmingham. On the return journey they carried Cannock coal. The canal for a generation monopolised trade and communication north from Worcester, and once operational the canal-side and the two basins came to be colonised by a variety of manufacturers.

It stimulated industrial enterprise down its 24-mile length, notably at Tardebigge with its lime- and brick-making kilns, and at Stoke Prior where salt springs were discovered in the bed of the newly-cut canal, prompting the digging of pits to extract brine, and the construction of salt-pans to refine the salt. Worcester itself attracted a variety of operations, drawn to the canal as a means of transporting finished products as well as a source of water and as a supplier of coal for fuel. *Royal Worcester Porcelain* (see Chapter 14), for example, built major works in the 1860s on the canal-side at Diglis, using the canal for its water supply and for importing china clay from Cornwall, coal from the Forest of Dean, and the lime and salt from Tardebigge and Stoke Prior necessary for glazing. Another porcelain works, that of *Grainger's*, built its factory at Lowesmoor, alongside coal and grain merchants, to take advantage of the canal.

Water was just as essential to the operations of the *Worcester Gaslight and Coke Company* and it too established itself at Lowesmoor within three years of the canal's opening. Gas lighting would illuminate and transform Victorian cities, and Worcester was in the vanguard; Bentley's *History of Worcester* records that in 1840 gas lighting 'was used in most places of worship, all the streets and squares, the principal shops, inns and public buildings and in many private dwellings'. The *Gaslight Company* needed water transport for the supply of coal to make coal-gas; lime was necessary to purify the gas. The by-products of the industrial process were coke, coal-tar and ammoniacal liquor which were sent downriver to Gloucester. But the Diglis Basin did accommodate its own rather unpleasant chemical process, that of treating Peruvian guano to make chemical manure, manufactured by *Webbs*, the industrial chemists; the canal was vital for Webbs' import and export trade.

Worcester's canal also enticed heavy industry, most notably *Hardy and Padmore*, whose founders established their first castings foundry barely two months after the canal opened. The waterway was critical to bring in coal and ore, and for subsequently moving the heavy castings which ranged from Westminster Embankment's dolphin lamp standards and the railway bridge at Foregate Street in Worcester to domestic ranges, grates, stoves and pots and pans, for which there was a truly national demand. Similarly, the *Vulcan* iron-works *(McKenzie and Holland)* had a factory on the tow-path between Cromwell Street and George Street; there it manufactured signal gantries and signalling equipment for the country's railway network and for export. But not every enterprise was concerned with the inedible; *Townshend's Mill* and silo, situated a few yards along the canal from the bottle kilns of the *Royal Worcester Porcelain Works*, was a substantial business which operated from the 1840s to the 1960s, bringing in grain up the Severn to be milled in a new steam-operated flour mill. The mill and silo were prominent features on Worcester's skyline until 1962. Again, this business illustrates the canal's virtuous trade cycle; coal borne down from Cannock, with flour carried back to bakeries and shops in Birmingham and the Black Country.

Cadbury Bros., the great Birmingham chocolate manufacturer, had used the Worcester and Birmingham Canal since the 1860s to bring coal, cocoa beans and sugar to its old Bridge Street factory in central Birmingham. In the late 1870s the business relocated to Bournville in Selly Oak and although it did use a rail link especially for coal, it developed canal-side facilities at Sparry's Wharf on the canal near Bournville. The advent of *Cadbury's Dairy Milk* at the start of the 20th century led to a dramatic increase in water-borne traffic. Initially milk was laboriously transported from Worcestershire dairy farms up the canal to Bournville, but the danger of milk curdling *en route* prompted the firm to open condensing plants, one of which was at Frampton-on-Severn. From 1915 a new process was initiated; chocolate crumb was brought to Frampton via the Worcester and Birmingham Canal and there mixed with sugar and condensed milk, dried and made into a new crumb which was carried back up to Bournville by barge; such was the volume of traffic that a much larger wharf was built in Bournville at 'Waterside', and from 1920 Worcester benefited directly when Cadbury's took over the Government's abandoned munitions factory at Blackpole which had its own canal-side wharf. Blackpole made wooden boxes and packing cases from timber brought in by river and canal, returning the finished items up the canal to Bournville. Later it would make cocoa tins and would prepare fruit and nuts for *Cadbury's* chocolate.

At its height the canal at Worcester was host to *Davenport's* brewery, to *Baldwin's* paper mill and to *Barker's* brick works which, at its Gregory's Bank manufactory on the east side of the canal at Worcester, pressed 1,500 bricks an hour for use in many of Worcester's public buildings. By the late 1960s most of these businesses had closed and fallen into dereliction. The canal itself had managed to fend off the threat from the railways in the latter part of the nineteenth century, but not that from road and lorry transport after 1945. Both Lowesmoor and Diglis Basins now went on to transform themselves into marinas, while the canal itself has been repaired and found a new life as the venue for pleasure trips and barge holidays. In fact, the nation-wide restoration of Britain's canals was inaugurated by a meeting at Tardebigge on Worcester's canal in 1946, which determined on the foundation of the Inland Waterways Association. It has recruited thousands of enthusiasts and volunteers across seventy years to help recover the glories of canals like that at Worcester which – in their time – had such a profound impact on the social and economic life of the country.

CHAPTER 14
Industrial Worcester

In the nineteenth and early twentieth centuries Worcester products were known right round the world. 'Worcester' porcelain, 'Worcestershire sauce', 'Worcester Pure Malt Vinegar', and Worcester's gloves were distinctive, of the finest quality, and were significant for their pre-eminent market position. Their factories clustered around the canal (see Chapter 13) or, later, around Shrub Hill railway station and Lowesmoor, with their railway links to Birmingham and London. But the long recessional of Worcester's industrial fortunes can be discerned from soon after the First World War; the glove industry subsequently relocated to Wiltshire, the vinegar and *Royal Worcester* factories eventually closed, and only *Lea and Perrins* with its inimitable sauce now survives in the city. Still – for decades – 'Worcester' was a manufacturing byword; this chapter is concerned with Worcester's industrial moment.

Although gloves first appear in Worcester records in the 13th century, and the Guild of Glovers was incorporated by warrant as early as 1497, the real impetus for Worcester's glove manufacture came around the time of the demise of the broadcloth industry in the 18th century; here was a ready-made skilled workforce. Apart from craft skills, Worcester had ready access to skins from Herefordshire and Shropshire, to the flowing water, lime and salt, essential for dressing the hides. The industry was further boosted by a change in late 18th-century fashion to the wearing of dress gloves (perhaps for cleanliness in an insanitary age) and by an Act of 1766 encouraging the import of unmanufactured kid and lamb skins. It was no coincidence that John Dent should establish his glove factory, precursor of *Dent Allcroft*, in 1777 because the times and Worcester's environment were propitious. By 1822 the foremost travelogue of the period, *Paterson's Roads*, was able to aver that: 'The principal manufactures of Worcester are those of a beautiful species of porcelain and of gloves, which are much approved and exported in large quantities.' The tower and sharply pointed spire of St Andrew's church, completed at the same time, is still known by locals as the Glover's Needle, a reminder of the industry's halcyon days.

Worcester was by 1825 indeed completely dominant in gloving in Britain, producing 620,000 dozen pairs of gloves, more than double the combined output of its nearest rivals Yeovil and Ludlow. Across the whole county of Worcestershire some 30,000 people were employed in the numerous stages of production in 150 glove manufactories. These involved preparing, feeding and softening the hides for tanning (washing, drying, paring, smoothing, sorting) before the most critical, most skilful, process of all – the cutting, the

Image produced by kind permission of Tudor House Museum from its Changing Face of Worcester collection- www.cfow.org.uk

Women workers at Fownes glove factory, *c*.1900.

male practitioners of which operation were the highest paid, having served a seven-year apprenticeship. Once cut, the pieces were farmed out to gloveresses who worked in colonies sewing, doing pointing and embroidery, and adding buttons (in St Martin's and St Peter's parishes, as well as in surrounding villages like Himbleton, Crowle and Suckley) before being returned to the factory for laying out and for glazing the seams. They were then packed and sent either to London for export to the colonies or USA, or they were sent to Birmingham, where merchants packed the gloves in barrels alongside other goods destined for export to Europe.

For the duration of the Napoleonic Wars, the British naval blockade of France ensured that *Dents* and other Worcester firms were largely unchallenged in both domestic and export markets; but peace in 1815 saw French manufacturers, who produced high-quality kid gloves, start to challenge Worcester's glovers in American markets. More damaging, however, was British legislation. William Huskisson, President of the Board of Trade, was seized by the desire to reduce barriers to free trade as part of a general liberalisation and, in 1824, ended the prohibition on imported gloves (among many other commodities). There followed a rapid collapse of Worcester's glove industry.

In 1831, such was the collapse in demand that *Dents* cut back on its labour costs. A petition to Parliament by 800 Worcester glove operatives urged the Commons to act to save the industry:

> Glove manufacture forms the chief resource of our city. Trade has circulated wealth and activity through other branches of our local commerce; its present distress and decay are bearing most heavily (on us).

The petitioners went on to cite figures: of every 1,000 male workers in Worcester, 113 were in full employment, 465 in partial employment, and 422 were unemployed. These economic difficulties provided the famous Victorian novelist Mrs Henry Wood with material for a portrait of Hestonleigh's (aka Worcester's) declining glove industry in her novel *Mrs Halliburton's Troubles*.

Nor was the industry helped by the fickleness of fashion, moving away from the stouter English glove to superfine kid gloves and to cotton substitutes. Increased competition therefore explains its rationalisation, as firms merged, and *Dent Allcroft* emerged in a dominant market position; only the arrival of *Fownes* from London in 1884 proved a challenge. Despite these economic difficulties even at the turn of the nineteenth century Worcester's gloving industry accounted for 20% of the male and 21.9% of the female workforce. The departure of *Dents* to Warminster in 1933, then its amalgamation with *Fownes*, which followed it to Wiltshire in 1974, effectively ended the city's direct involvement with firms which even now continue to make a high-quality product elsewhere in the country. Only the Fownes Hotel, imaginatively rejuvenating the old Fownes factory buildings in Lowesmoor, is a reminder of an illustrious past.

We saw that *Paterson's Roads* in 1822 praised the excellence of Worcester's porcelain; it was by then a well-established industry. The city's position on the Severn was important, for the waterway made for easy movement of heavy and bulky raw materials. Just as important was the human factor – Dr John Wall and William Davis, a physician and an apothecary, respectively conducted experiments from 1750 in porcelain-making and succeeded in utilising Cornish soap-rock to make a durable porcelain. Their partnership, *Worcester Tonquin Manufactory*, then proceeded to find the financial backing for new works at Warmstry on the banks of Worcester's Severn, upriver from the Cathedral. At the outset it developed transfer printing of the highest quality, which John Sandon, in his book *Worcester Porcelain*, says 'was probably Worcester's greatest contribution to the ceramics industry'. The firm produced the world's first commemorative mug, that of the King of Prussia, Frederick the Great, a popular figure in England as for long he was a foremost ally in our Continental wars.

Still, financial troubles beset them from early on and Thomas Flight had to rescue the firm, helped by the fortuitous visit of George III to *Flight's* shop on High Street in 1788; Valentine Green recorded that 'the king, being of a mechanical turn and fond of seeing manufactories of all sorts', spent two hours visiting the shop while staying at the Bishop's Palace to attend the Three Choirs Festival. The king was very impressed with Worcester ware and suggested Flight open a shop in London, which he did. Green commented that this 'shop was liberally honoured by different branches of the royal family'. Flight, and his partner Barr, specialised in elegant tea sets and extensive services, and increasingly in vases, painted with a degree of realism (for example, in the depiction of bird's feathers) unequalled in English porcelain. This was because *Flight and Barr* attracted some of England's finest porcelain painters to their factory, and then encouraged them to consider each item as if it were 'a piece of jewellery'.

Flight and Barr was by no means the only porcelain factory in Worcester. By 1800 Robert Chamberlain, who had worked at *Flight's*, had established his own High Street shop and a factory at Diglis (handily placed for the imminent arrival of a canal link to the Midlands). In 1796, when Green was completing his *History*, he commented that 'the manufactory is in rapid progress towards perfection'. Chamberlain had his own famous patron, for Lord Nelson, with Emma Hamilton on his one good arm, and her cuckolded husband in tow, visited the factory in 1802 and ordered a complete dinner service, which sadly Nelson never lived to see. He had visited the Chamberlains because of their reputation for very fine decorative work, especially 'their uncommonly rich gilding'. But by 1840 Chamberlain's successors had taken over *Flight and Barr*; Warmstry would become a factory for coarse ceramic tiles, and production of fine pieces would be focused on Diglis, where the distinctive bottle-kilns reared up by the side of the Worcester and Birmingham Canal. The business was now known as *Royal Worcester Porcelain* in recognition of George III's early patronage. Here, in the words of the historian of ceramics, John Sandon: 'Worcester craftsmen created some of the finest porcelain sculptures, the like of which are unlikely (sic) to be made again.' Nevertheless, the business evolved, and adapted – perhaps too slowly – to changing tastes. Under the leadership of Richard Binns in the second half of the 19th century the company continued to lead the ceramic world with fine enamelled figures and vases, but it also mastered Japanese, Chinese, Indian and Persian styles, feeding a seemingly insatiable Victorian demand for exotic curiosities, with which the middle and upper classes filled their homes.

The Edwardian period saw a dramatic change in taste to Art Nouveau and Art Deco styles; *Royal Worcester Porcelain* took time to adjust. By now it had absorbed the remaining independent porcelain company in Worcester: *Graingers* of St Martin's Gate in Lowesmoor, long-term specialists in semi-porcelain (which is earthen-ware rather than true porcelain) and in chemical porcelain, a product for laboratory work, was now failing commercially. Soon enough *Royal Worcester* found that it too was in difficulties, for its richly decorated and costly pieces increasingly fell out of fashion; furthermore, the post-1918 Depression rendered them unaffordable for most. It was thanks to the philanthropy of Charles Dyson Perrins, a connoisseur and collector of its porcelain, that the company was saved; after loans and gifts, he eventually bought the whole operation, being involved with it for a total of 57 years. Latterly the company was successful in producing one of the most popular sets of tableware in the post-War period, *Evesham Gold*, decorated as it was with the indigenous fruits of the Vale to the south of Worcester and with the gold band which recalled the company's early reputation for gilding. Even this was insufficient to prevent first merger with *Spode*, then the cessation of production at Worcester in 2009, even though – as part of the Portmeirion Group – its name would live on elsewhere in the production of luxury tableware.

Worcester was long famed for its condiments. *Hill, Evans and Co. Ltd* was established in the centre of Worcester in 1830 by William Hill and Edward Evans, two enterprising chemists, initially to produce vinegar. At their six-acre site at Lowesmoor they built the Great Filling Hall which housed the world's largest vat, capable of holding *c.*115 gallons of vinegar. The label on the bottle proclaimed that *Hill, Evans and Co. Ltd's* Pure Malt Vinegar came from 'Worcester', where the Lowesmoor factory was the largest vinegar works in the world, capable of producing two million gallons a year. Such was the volume of traffic that the works were served from 1870 by their very own 'Vinegar Works' branch railway line, sometimes known as the Lowesmoor Tramway, a purpose-built extension of the national rail network from Worcester Shrub Hill station where it joined the Midland Railway and the Oxford, Worcester and Wolverhampton Railway. For more than a century *Hill, Evans and Co. Ltd.* competed strongly in the world's vinegar market; but by 1965 economic pressures had forced its closure, only the Great Filling Hall, now a Territorial Army headquarters, surviving as a relic of a once-thriving industry.

The most famous, and durable, condiment of all was *Lea and Perrins Worcester Sauce*. Just like *Hill, Evans and Co. Ltd* this was a product conceived in the 1830s by two chemists or druggists, John Lea from Feckenham and William Perrins from Chaddesley Corbett. They were partners in a chemist's shop in Broad Street which stocked over 300 items, including medicinal herbs, leaves, fruit and roots, and which manufactured its own preparations, like Dover's Powder, Tartar Emetic, Liver Pills and Turkey Rhubarb. The partners also specialised in making and stocking medical chests, for the home market as well as for

The 'Vinegar Express'. Locomotive on the Lowesmoor Tramway.

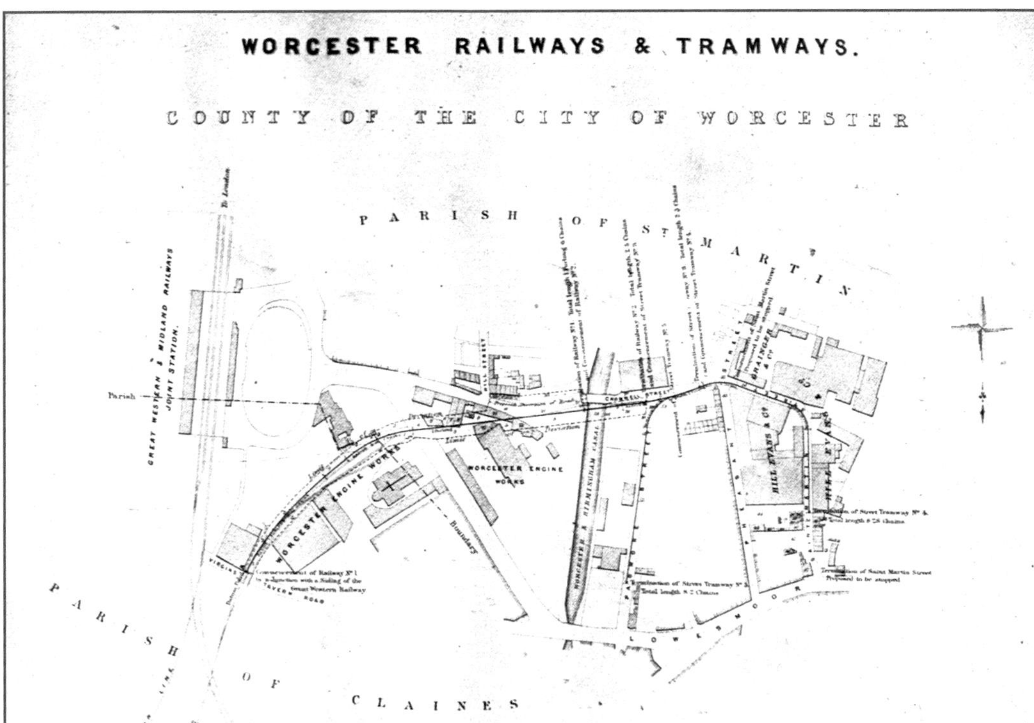

Plan of the Lowesmoor Tramway, also known as the Vinegar Works Branch, as it served the Hill & Evans Vinegar Works.

travellers, replete with bottles, herbs, pills, pestle and mortar and medical apparatus. By 1840 this business in medical chests extended round the world. And by then the partnership was changing to accommodate a new product, and what would become an even bigger global market.

According to tradition the famous sauce was first blended in 1837, a mix of malt vinegar, spirit vinegar, molasses, salt, sugar, anchovies, tamarind, shallots, garlic and sundry sauces and flavouring; it was made to a secret recipe vouchsafed by 'A Nobleman of the County'. The intriguing recipe, and the equally intriguing 'nobleman', have of course given rise to continued speculation. It seems that the common assumption that the latter was Marcus, Lord Sandys, former Governor of Bengal, does not stand up to close scrutiny even if the sauce itself does betray a distinctive Oriental, indeed Indian, character. It is alleged that the nameless nobleman came into the shop in 1837 and asked that a bottle of this sauce be made up for him; that Messrs. Lea and Perrins made an extra jar for themselves, then consigned it to the cellar, and only on opening it months later found to their pleasant surprise that it had matured and become very palatable. Even now the product is given several years to mature in the bottle before being dispatched.

At first the back-room of the shop on Broad Street, later extended to include a bigger laboratory, was used as manufactory for the sauce. In the 1890s a much larger site was acquired on Midland Road, close to the Midland and the Oxford, Worcester and Wolverhampton Railway lines at Shrub Hill station. This business expansion was prompted by strong demand round the world as the firm's representatives in both the British Empire and the USA established contacts and racked up sales. The idiosyncratic packaging – long-necked medicine-style bottles, deep orange labels densely packed with illustrations, information and claims of medical efficacy – helped those sales immeasurably. Foremost among those claims was the assertion that the sauce 'was acknowledged to contribute to health by stomachic and digestive qualities'. Sales were assisted too by association with the home city – *Lea and Perrins* fought hard through the law courts to repel rivals, from the middle of the 19th century, who would appropriate the epithet 'Worcestershire Sauce.' Finally, much mileage was made from stories which demonstrated the product's enduring quality; so, the recovery of a *Lea and Perrins* bottle in 1989 from the wreck of the *Kyarra*, sunk by a U-boat off Swanage in 1918, was rendered more newsworthy when it was opened, tested, and found to be both completely unaffected by its 70-year immersion and still very palatable. Thanks to the legend that has grown up around their product *Lea and Perrins* – if under different ownership – flourishes still, the sole remaining representative in the city itself of those distinctive Worcester products from its industrial age.

CHAPTER 15

Edward Elgar

Worcester City

Edward Elgar (1857-1934). This portrait of the city's famous musician hangs in the Guildhall.

Edward Elgar (1857-1934) was the greatest British composer since Henry Purcell, two hundred years before him. His *Enigma Variations*, first performed in 1899, marked the beginning of a major revival in English music which had languished for decades. A few years later his *Symphony No.1* – performed 82 times in one calendar year (1908) in Germany, Austria and St Petersburg, and as far afield as Australia and America – established him as much more than an insular, but as an international, composer of real stature. His musical voice was distinctive and instantly recognisable, reflecting the fact that he was self-taught, free from academy convention. It also expressed considerable personal complexity, both in his instinctive and almost euphoric response to martial pomp and pageantry but also in an occasionally crippling sense of insecurity, regret and dissatisfaction with his lot in life.

Although to some he became the embodiment of a smug jingoism, for his compositions, the *Pomp and Circumstance Military Marches, Cockaigne (In London Town),* and *Coronation Ode* coincided with the high summer of Britain's Imperial mission, he was very much more than that. His two *Symphonies*, the *Dream of Gerontius* and his *Cello and Violin Concertos,* for example, reveal profound emotional depths, sincerity and power. But it was the mystery of the *Enigma Variations* and those patriotic marches which made him widely popular; Vaughan Williams later wrote that 'it falls to the lot of very few composers to achieve this bond of unity with their countrymen'. He also became a society darling which ensured he would be decorated with signal honours, created a baronet, be awarded the Order of Merit, be elevated to the position of Master of the King's Musick, and garner honorary degrees from the ancient universities; in all this he was beating a new path for English musicians who followed him. Still, however much he exulted in the Establishment's recognition in London, his heart remained – all his life – in Worcester and the Worcestershire countryside he walked and cycled in his youth.

Born in Broadheath (three miles outside Worcester) in 1857, Edward Elgar thereafter spent the next forty years or so living in the heart of the city, where his father (an able amateur musician) was both a piano-tuner to the Worcestershire great and good, and the owner of a music shop. He accompanied his father on his visits to the county's aristocratic piles (tradesman's entrance only), watching him piano-tuning there, and in the organ-loft of St George's Roman Catholic church in Worcester, where William Elgar was organist. The young Elgar was given violin lessons but in other ways he was an autodidact, poring over textbooks and scores in the music shop. He evidently had great natural talent, for those who later observed him working talked of his prodigious compositional skill, while he himself averred that his music flowed out of him, apparently unmediated and uncorrected, straight onto the manuscript page.

The Worcester environment did much to shape his musical ideas; firstly, St George's where he learnt to play the organ and was eventually to succeed his rather indolent father as organist. In addition, the Anglican Cathedral in the city was to have an enduring effect on him. He later said: 'My first music was learnt in the Cathedral from books borrowed from the music library when I was eight, nine or ten.' There he listened to as much music as he could, hearing the choir sing Byrd, Tallis and Purcell, as well as attending the Three Choirs Festival when the Cathedral was hosting. Experiencing Handel's *Messiah* performed in 1869 when he was twelve years old inspired him to reach new heights playing his violin. Perhaps the single most influential Festival moment was in 1884 when Elgar, playing in the first violins, experienced the 'ravishing, tuneful, clever orchestration' (as he put it) of Dvorak's *Symphony No. 6*, in a performance conducted by the composer himself. The Cathedral would be closely associated with him all his life; of the mature Elgar the *Manchester Guardian*'s music critic would later write that 'the very walls of the Cathedral cry out to us from the same romantic past that bred his music. His music, heard within them, is redolent of England'.

He benefited too from what David Cannadine in a stimulating essay, *Orchestrating His Own Life; Sir Edward Elgar as an Historical Personality*, termed 'the vigorous associational life of the city'. He threw himself into local music-making, joining the Glee Club, playing initially with the second violins in Worcester's Philharmonic Society before becoming its leader, performing in the attendants' band at the County of Worcester Lunatic Asylum, becoming director of the Worcester Instrumental Society for the Cultivation of Instrumental Music (1877) and, near the turn of the century, founding the Worcestershire Philharmonic, which he conducted until 1904. Worcester gave him the opportunity to compose, and to get his work performed. He started with motets for St George's when he was fifteen; he moved on to wind quintets and quadrilles in his late teens and then fuller orchestral pieces, but by the end of the 1880s there was a danger he would be destined to remain a peripatetic violin teacher, and a local organist and choir master, were it not for the fact that in his *Ave Verum Corpus* (which has remained a popular church anthem ever since) and in

Image produced by kind permission of Tudor House Museum from its Changing Face of Worcester collection- www.cfow.org.uk

The Firs, Elgar's birthplace at Lower Broadheath, near Worcester.

his *Serenade for Strings* he was beginning to show signs of his considerable talent. That was becoming more widely recognised, and the Worcester Festival committee in 1890 commissioned an orchestral work, *Froissart*, which gave an early demonstration of his exceptional ability to orchestrate, of a different order from any British contemporaries. As Elgar's friend, William Reed wrote: 'He knew unerringly what he wanted in the way of orchestral or choral tone, balance and colour'.

The next decade saw the Festival continue to give him opportunities to refine his compositional craft, and he progressed to writing choral works too, with oratorios first performed in Worcester – *The Black Knight* (1893) and *Lux Christi (The Light of Life)* (1896), for example. And if his greatest choral work *The Dream of Gerontius* was commissioned and first performed (disastrously) elsewhere – in Birmingham in 1900 – it was in Worcester, with his own

Worcestershire Philharmonic, that the first successful British performance was given in May 1901. Now his countrymen could begin to appreciate it as 'one of the most remarkable, beautiful and impressive works ever written by an English composer', as Michael Kennedy, his biographer, put it. Even if fame and fortune took him to London at the turn of the century, twenty years later he would return to Worcestershire to live, and to re-engage with the local music scene.

Worcester and the surrounding county gave him his musical breaks but in other ways too, his background there deeply influenced him. Cannadine's 'vigorous associational life' equally applies, in his own words, to the city's 'burgeoning civic consciousness, civic pride, civic pageantry'. imitative of London's own royal displays. And Elgar seems to have responded enthusiastically to the military ceremonial and the soldiers' parades of the Worcestershire regiment, the flags and the bunting, in sum all the flummery and ornamentation celebrating a nation still – at the turn of the century – intoxicated with the Imperial dream. It helped that Worcester had been solidly Unionist since 1886 and close to Birmingham, the epicentre of Unionism, where Joseph Chamberlain articulated the vision of an Empire centred on Britain and bound together by Imperial preference. Elgar was a Tory all his life. Out of his pride in national pageantry and display came the colourful, tuneful, invigorating music, like *Land of Hope and Glory,* the other *Pomp and Circumstance Marches* and *Cockaigne*, so loved by millions of Edwardians.

Just beyond the city, the surrounding countryside comprised for him a pastoral idyll all his days, for though he did not always have a home in the city, he would live close by it, as, for example, at Malvern Wells in the 1890s, and he engaged in country pursuits like walking, beagling and fishing into his old age. When he resided in London in the years of his greatest popularity, he was homesick for Worcestershire, telling a friend in 1912: 'I long for a sight of my own country.' The death of his wife in April 1920 accentuated that longing and he wrote to an intimate: 'I like to think of the Worcester days, and you and the flowers and the fruit and the warm sun and my cathedral and my music – but it is lonely.' In truth he was fully aware that it was only really in Worcestershire that he could find the peace and quiet he needed to work effectively. It was an inspiration to him in his music, most obviously in one of his first significant choral works *Caractacus* (1898), which told of the last British stand against the Romans in the Malvern Hills. But just as much, the friends he made there were to be immortalised in the *Enigma Variations*, that orchestral work which first announced the arrival of a genuine talent on the British music scene. The subjects of the individual variations on a central theme comprised, among others, a Worcestershire country squire, a Malvern architect, the chatelaine of Madresfield, local ladies from the Worcestershire Philharmonic Society, a chamber music crony from Worcester, and a member of a Malvern musical family.

Yet for all that he loved his home city and the county, another side of him resented its parochialism. It irked him that he should have spent so long marking time in Worcester – some forty years – before national recognition. He was conscious, too, of being a bit of an outsider – a Catholic and a provincial with a lower middle-class background, the son of a tradesman; in 1900 he was to say to a friend that 'I know I was kept out of everything decent 'cos (my) father keeps a shop'. Perhaps this is why he worked so hard to impress royalty, dedicating works to the monarchy from Queen Victoria and on to the *Nursery Suite* for the young princesses, Elizabeth and Margaret Rose in 1931, whilst also making himself a favourite of Edward VII. It also explains his unquenchable desire for honours, and even in his last years, after all his many decorations, he was still campaigning for his elevation to the peerage. His lack of formal musical training made him chippy about academic composers like Stanford and Parry; Stanford's Cambridge snobbery and exclusivity gave him good cause at times. Elgar thus took particular pleasure in the veritable shower of honorary doctorates accorded him around 1900, taking the robes of his Cambridge doctorate at the first opportunity back to Worcester to show his proud parents. He might fulminate against the music establishment, but he craved its recognition; the Mastership of the King's Musick consolidated his position among the leading musicians of his day.

Where Stanford, Parry and later English composers like Britten, Walton and Tippett were highly educated and well off, Elgar was conscious both of his comparative educational deprivation (taught in a dame school in Worcester, then in Spetchley Roman Catholic school) and of his family's relatively modest financial circumstances. It made him intensely conscious of money once his compositions started to achieve success. It would be churlish to suggest he married Alice Roberts (daughter of Major-General Sir Henry Roberts) because she was a lady of means, but that marriage made him financially secure, even if his treatment at the hands of those relatives who disapproved of her marrying trade only reinforced his consciousness of being an outsider. When the commissions came in and he was successful, he enjoyed the money, spending freely on their London home (Severn House – note the allusion) and on an extensive social life in the capital.

Perhaps financial security partly explains the dulling of his creative spark. For, after that concentration of great works which established his reputation from the *Variations, Gerontius, The Kingdom* and the *Violin Concerto* the pace slowed. Even in the First World War he still managed to write *The Spirit of England* and his marvellous *Cello Concerto*, but his last fifteen years were largely barren. There would be one last hurrah, the *Severn Suite* for brass band, and later for orchestra, dedicated to various locations in his beloved Worcester (Castle, Cathedral and Commandery), and premiered at the Three Choirs Festival in the city in 1932. It was not simply that the commercial imperative had faded. Just as importantly the First World War and its revolutionary consequences deeply affected him, not simply through the human cost but just as importantly because of the destruction of a whole pre-war civilisation – balmy Edwardian summer gave place to spiritual winter after 1918. Martial pomp and swagger seemed both unfashionable and tasteless, and that side of his output tended to colour a wider appreciation of his music.

Elgar's own appearance had anachronistic echoes; photographs from the 1920s and 1930s show him in the guise of the country squire or, whenever the occasion allowed, sporting full academic dress or gartered and velvet-clad decorated with his stars and sashes and his honours. To some he seemed out of time, an Edwardian relic. But not in Worcester, where he was still revered and where he took an active part in civic and musical life and continued to conduct in the Three Choirs Festival memorably, almost up to his death in 1934. He died in Worcester in Marl Bank in 1934, the city hosting the national memorial service shortly afterwards. The bronze statue opposite the Cathedral, and the stained-glass window in the Cathedral itself, memorialise one of Worcester's favourite and most famous sons, the local man who led the renaissance of English music in the twentieth century and whose compositions to this day, more than those of any other musician, popularly embody the emotions of patriotic pride and fervour.

Chapter 15

Worcester and the Three Choirs Festival

© Illustrated London News Ltd/Mary Evans

Crowds line the Cathedral for the Three Choirs Festival, 1848.

The Three Choirs Festival is one of the oldest classical choral festivals in the world and although there has been debate about the precise date of the first gathering of Worcester, Gloucester and Hereford Cathedral musicians, the present organisers confidently announced that 2019 would see the 292nd Festival. This annual festival has rotated between the three cities and from the outset performed choral music, with Purcell, especially the *Te Deum* and *Jubilate*, and Handel *(Samson, Judas Maccabeus* and *Messiah)* prominent in eighteenth century programming. By 1788 its reputation was such that the King, George III, who had been taking the waters at Cheltenham on the advice of his physician, determined to come to the Festival, had it re-scheduled, took up residence at the Bishop's Palace close to Worcester's Cathedral, and attended a memorable performance of the *Messiah*. It was the first time the nave was used for the Festival, with the royal party in a specially constructed gallery, 'spread with a rich Worcester carpet, lined and faced with crimson silk, and shaded with a lofty canopy surmounted with a crown'. under the Great West Window. The nave itself was filled with seats.

In September 1830 Princess Victoria, heir to the throne, attended the Worcester Festival, the local newspaper the *Worcester Herald* recording the visit unctuously as 'an opportunity of evincing that loyalty and attachment to the Royal Family, for which this city has at all times been so conspicuous'. A cavalcade of bishops, nobility and local worthies accompanied Their Royal Highnesses, the Duchess of Kent (mother of the heir) and Princess Victoria, to the special elevated compartment constructed for them right by Prince Arthur's Chapel, and heard the choir sing 'When thou hadst overcome the sharpness of death…' to an accompanying thunderstorm at the Opening Service.

By now Festival programmes included Haydn's popular *The Creation* and Mendelssohn's *Elijah* was for decades an annual fixture, a reflection of the esteem with which the composer was held in Victorian England. These works were performed to much larger audiences than a century earlier, a consequence of the coming of the railways which enabled devotees to travel from further afield. That popularity offended some puritanical churchmen and in 1874 the very future of the Festival in Worcester was placed in jeopardy as Dean, Chapter and wealthy local Lord Dudley determined on discontinuing the Festival in the Cathedral on the grounds that oratorios profaned the sacred ecclesiastical space. Public indignation, appeals to the Queen, and widespread mockery in the Press and in the musical world forced the capitulation of the Chapter the following year, with the introduction of prayers before every performance providing some small consolation for clerical hard-liners.

Increasingly in the late nineteenth century the Three Choirs Festival became a celebration of English music. Edward Elgar's compositions were increasingly seen as a highpoint of Festival Week, and Elgar became particularly associated with the Worcester Festival; indeed, the Festival and the composer remain inextricably linked. Elgar inspired others: Ralph Vaughan Williams premiered his *Fantasia on a Theme of Thomas Tallis* in Gloucester in 1910 and his *Five Mystical Songs* in Worcester the following year. Through the twentieth century the works of Herbert Howells and Gerald Finzi received their first performances, and those of English composers like Britten, Holst, Walton and Parry regularly featured, while great choral classics by J S Bach, Mozart, Haydn and Handel continue to be performed annually to large numbers of enthusiasts.

CHAPTER 16

Worcester's Electoral Notoriety

Edwardian Worcester impinged on the national consciousness for another reason, apart from those intimate links with its famous musical son, Edward Elgar. In 1906 the city achieved real notoriety, becoming proverbial for corruption as a result of its conduct of the General Election contest; the behaviour of its politicians prompted the appointment of a Royal Commission to inquire into the *Existence of Corrupt Practices at the last Election for the City of Worcester*. The leading historian of British Elections in this period, Henry Pelling, identified what he called a 'rock bottom list of constituencies where a proportion of the voters was purchased at no less than one General Election', made up of perhaps a dozen boroughs. Along with Exeter, Ipswich, Norwich, Rochester and Shrewsbury, he included Worcester. As Lloyd George pointed out 'corruption seems to be common in the cathedral cities'; but few of them endured the penetrative probing of that Royal Commission as Worcester did – the city was distinguished even in a rogues' gallery comprising that 'rock bottom list'.

Mary Evans Picture Library

George Allsopp, MP for Worcester 1885-1906.

The popular image of nineteenth-century elections has been shaped by Charles Dickens' fictional account of the aptly named Eatanswill election in his *Pickwick Papers* (1836). Until the Ballot Act was passed in 1872, ending the open casting of votes and insisting instead on a secret ballot, elections were often much as Dickens portrayed them, boisterous affairs involving a degree of physical persuasion to secure the votes. Even after 1872 malpractice was common, and it reached unacceptable levels in 1880, when the conduct of the election prompted 'a widespread feeling of shame and humiliation at the scandalous disclosures' (Kathryn Rix, 'The Elimination of Corrupt Practices in British Elections'). There were more election petitions to Parliament in 1880 (39) requesting that the result of the recent contest be overturned than at any time since 1832, and 15 were successful. Royal Commissions named 9,000 people they found guilty of corrupt practices; the shocking fact was that in their number were magistrates, aldermen, councillors and industrialists, and that both parties, Liberal and Conservative, were equally culpable.

Sir Henry James, the new Liberal Attorney General, introduced an important bill in 1881 to eliminate 'Corrupt and Illegal Practices'. saying: 'We have sat long enough on the bank, but the stream of corruption flows on and it seems useless to hope that it will cease to flow unless something is done to stop it'. He then anatomised that 'stream of corruption'. One manifestation was that of 'colourable employment' where voters in their hundreds were paid for doing very little; Rix cites the example of Oxford where in a seat with *c.* 6,000 voters the Liberals employed 78 clerks, 15 canvassers, 190 messengers and 106 detectives(!). One might equally point to Sandwich (the subject of a Royal Commission in 1880) where hundreds were employed to erect flagpoles or simply to witness the unfurling and furling of banners.

Some constituencies lovingly perpetuated rotten borough practices from the start of the 19th century, when there was an expectation that voters would be paid for their vote. In many more this purchase of votes was effected by the open-handed generosity of candidates in treating voters to drink in the constituency's pubs (a 'torrent of gin and beer', as Gladstone put it in 1874). By 1880 there was a larger electorate because the 1867 Reform Act had extended the vote to borough householders; now, fighting an election was an exorbitantly expensive affair. In reality, members of both parties welcomed a bill to limit the expense. James's Corrupt Practices Act, eventually passed in 1883, increased penalties for bribery, treating, using undue influence and personation (impersonating another voter at the ballot box); it also brought in strict limits to spending on agents, clerks, committee rooms (hitherto candidates might hire rooms in every city pub, there to hold court and dispense alcoholic largesse), on conveyances to take voters to the polls, and finally, on banners, posters and some other printed materials.

It has been widely assumed that this Act transformed Britain's electoral story, historians writing complacently that 'it was a landmark in the development of democracy in England' (Seymour), and that 'Parliament managed within one generation to sweep away traditions that were centuries old' (O'Leary). And it is true that the number of petitions to Parliament challenging election results after 1883 fell, though this might be because the outcome was uncertain and because local voters often later resented petitioner-candidates who could not take defeat uncomplainingly. Just as importantly, at times both sides were equally guilty of malpractice and to challenge a result might be to open oneself up to a persuasive counter-charge.

The Act was also a landmark in the great

momentum it applied to the party-political evolution of voluntary helpers – canvassers, pamphleteers or fund-raisers. The Conservatives' million-strong Primrose League (1883 onwards) and Joseph Chamberlain's army of volunteers (including women) in his Liberal Unionist and Tariff Reform organisations exemplify this. Finally, the sort of flagrant abuses that had pertained before 1883 evidently now diminished, partly because the 1884 Franchise Act widened the electorate still further, so increasing the number of voters in many places that bribery was impractical; and partly because the 1885 Redistribution Act swept away many of the remaining small, corruptible boroughs which had still survived after 1832.

Yet the narrative that 1883 represents a wholesale transformation has to be qualified. Corruption did not cease, and Worcester proves it. It was one of those 'especially vulnerable small boroughs, cathedral cities, maritime and riparian constituencies'; its vulnerability may have lain in the relatively small number of voters (8,000) or in the reliance of the voting poor on church charities. The modest size of its electorate meant that, although it had sent two representatives to Parliament from the time of Edward I, it lost one member in the shake-up of Parliamentary boundaries in 1885. For the next twenty years its sole seat returned a Conservative candidate, even bucking the national trend in 1906 when, outside the West Midlands, there was a Liberal landslide. For most of those twenty years a whiff of corruption attached itself to the city, which is why the Liberals petitioned Parliament in 1892 against the election of the Hon. George Allsopp (who had held the seat since 1885). They alleged 147 cases of bribery with money, 93 with drink, 28 through illegal employment and 67 cases of general treating. If true, these were major and multiple infractions of the 1883 Act.

The justices giving judgement on the petition were lenient, believing the best of George Allsopp. They found 'nothing approaching to general illegality or corruption to be proved... for the evidence in support is very slender indeed'. Whilst there 'was no manner of doubt' that buying rounds of drinks (treating) by Allsopp's agent – Mr Bowen – took place, it was impossible to prove intention. 'No man could abstain from hospitality when an election is pending,' they concluded. They made much of the fact that it would be quite wrong to unseat the MP on the unverifiable and dubious evidence of corruption presented by the petitioners. But they also concluded that Allsopp's electoral agent, 'himself in giving evidence gave the impression that he was the sort of man who had no objection to bribery or treating'. While Allsopp survived, a taint of sleaze still clung to the city's Conservative politicians. Nor did the good people of Worcester appear grateful to those crusading for clean elections; the solicitor who handled the petition in 1892 was burnt in effigy for his pains. After all, why would one tolerate the threatened derailment of one's gravy train?

Still, the equivocal conclusion of the 1892

Worcester City

George Henry Williamson, whose election as Worcester MP was subject to a Royal Commission which found evidence of corruption.

enquiry unquestionably influenced the Commissioners as they came to investigate the circumstances surrounding the 1906 General Election. This time the election of Allsopp's successor, George Williamson (Conservative) – by the slender margin of 129 votes – faced legal challenge. The Royal Commission report records that 'sufficient evidence was given us to convince us that both before and since 1892 corrupt practices at both Parliamentary and Municipal Elections in Worcester have systematically prevailed'. A certain Mr William Leicester, a reliable and experienced member of the political class in the city, as well as a performer in the youthful Elgar's wind quintet, gave evidence to the Commissioners of 'the existence of a bribable class in Worcester…and from his experience in the city, no election at Worcester could be won except by bribery. (He considered) that corruption was greater now than formerly'. The Commission 'took considerable pains to calculate the probable number of persons forming this 'bribable class'. We are of opinion that 500 may be accepted as approximately correct'.

Several aspects of the Conservatives' behaviour in the 1906 Election campaign exercised the Commissioners. They noted how the National Conservative League, set up for political, educational and social purposes, spawned ten lodges in Worcester to which members paid a low annual subscription (1/-), in turn benefiting from periodical smoking concerts. 'The Chairman usually paid for the whole company's drinks. It was proved to us that persons other than members of the League could obtain admission to these concerts'. This custom had subsisted back in 1892 when the leading judge had then resolved that 'the practice by which the president of the evening has paid at its conclusion for the drinks round…is objectionable, demoralising and dangerous to the seat'. Subsequent (perhaps half-hearted) efforts to eradicate the tradition had not met with much success. It seemed clear by 1906 that 'treating' in contravention of the act of 1883 was still going on.

To obtain proof that the Conservatives were also involved in the bribery of voters, the Liberals planted spies to watch the operations of the Conservative Party in Worcester. Because Conservatives had some inkling of this, the extent of their misconduct may have been contained; and because the Liberals were transparent in their commitment to running their own campaign free from any corruption at all, this had the effect of reducing the individual amounts expended in bribery – voters could not persuade the two sides to outbid each other! The Commission found 'a uniformity in amount of each bribe – about 2s 6d to an individual voter' – and concluded that there was 'organised bribery and treating', though it was unable conclusively 'to trace the source of the funds'. In reams of evidence to the judges a depressing picture emerged of feckless voters persuaded to take a couple of shillings (for example, left discreetly on the wall outside a public house) in return for their votes.

However, 'a grave suspicion as to the source' focused on Walter Caldicott, a personal friend of Williamson's and one of the leaders of the Conservative Party in Worcester. Soon after Williamson's adoption as the party candidate Caldicott received a cheque from him for £100 which he paid into an 'Election Expenses account'. 'Ultimately, by cheques or payments in cash, it found its way to a man called Thornborrow, the salaried Secretary of the Conservative Association. On the night of 27 December (in the midst of the bitterly fought election campaign), and after the receipt of several sums from Caldicott, this Thornborrow was found drunk and disorderly in the streets of Worcester with £14 in his possession.' He was quite unable to explain what the £14 was for. Although convicted, and fined the next day, he continued to receive money from Caldicott.

The Commission 'endeavoured to obtain from Caldicott and Thornborrow an account of the way the £100 was expended'. The latter produced a memorandum book but this it transpired 'had been mutilated by having pages torn from it'; he claimed he had torn them out in Caldicott's presence and handed them over to him. Caldicott denied all knowledge of this; nor could he produce the counterfoils for the cheques made out to Charles Thornborrow. When tasked with evidence that in at least one case the counterfoil of a cheque was carefully excised from the cheque book, to leave no trace of its existence (save to someone following the sequence of counterfoil numbers), Caldicott claimed it was for a personal and private matter he did not wish to disclose, fuelling speculation that this was either a romantic, or politically disreputable, affair.

This saga of obfuscation and evasion convinced the Commission that Williamson's £100 payment to Caldicott and 'its distribution through Thornborrow was an illegal practice'. At the going rate of 2s 6d per vote, £100 carefully targeted could purchase up to 800 votes, quite enough to swing the result in Worcester. Thornborrow had lubricated his drinking companions on 27 December and the suspicion must be that direct payments supplemented that hospitality. In its quietly devastating conclusion, the Commission reiterated:

> That there exists in Worcester a class of voters numbering approximately 500 and consisting mainly of the needy and loafing class, but including a considerable number of working men in regular employment who are prepared to sell their votes for drink or money.

It went on to particularise in four schedules attached to the report, publishing a long list which identified named individuals found guilty of bribery and/or treating. Caldicott and Thornborrow had a schedule all to themselves, and both were found guilty 'of an illegal practice', though they were subsequently furnished with certificates of indemnity so that they avoided a jail sentence. The judgement overturned the 1906 result, voiding Williamson's election because he was guilty 'by his agents of the corrupt practice of bribery'.

Two years elapsed before a by-election was held to return a replacement for George Williamson and during that time the failure of the Liberal government to issue a writ for a new election was hotly debated in the House of Commons. Liberal MPs and ministers argued that Worcester's electors were guilty of corruption and must have a period of reflection on the wickedness of their ways before another election; Conservatives countered that it was wrong that the actions of a small minority should deny a large majority their proper representation.

When the by-election was fought in 1908, Worcester's electors, agents and candidates seem to have learnt their lesson; there was no recurrence of those corrupt and illegal practices. But as Pelling wryly put it: 'The Liberals had to bear the odium of having publicised the whole matter – and of having cut off a regular source of income for the needy.' Indeed, they were deeply unpopular after 1906, with leading Liberals being burnt in effigy which, in light of what also happened in 1892, was clearly something of a regional specialism. A local paper carried a poem which included the lines:

> We're going to burn in effigy,
> Them blokes who wants to interfere,
> Between a poor man and his beer,
> Upon election day.

Conservatives constantly harked back to the Liberals' 1906 petition, and some prominent Liberals subsequently suffered vindictive treatment, including the loss of their employment. The Conservatives campaigned to great effect; in that 1908 contest they recorded their highest majority (1,292) since 1885, and they went on to secure comfortable victories in the two General Elections of 1910. The Liberals learnt that – in Worcester in any case – virtuous behaviour was no guarantee of a grateful electorate.

CHAPTER 17

The Battle of Gheluvelt, 31 October 1914

The Worcestershire Regiment, though originally founded in 1694, had from 1881 been based at Norton Barracks, a prominent landmark built in the Fortress Gothic Revival style on the southern edge of the city. It recruited from Worcester itself, as well as from the two counties of Herefordshire and Worcestershire. A number of those who fought in the Ypres campaign of October 1914 hailed from Worcester city. When the First World War broke out the city became a centre for recruiting troops to be dispatched to Belgium and France.

The Worcestershire Regiment was to be involved very early in the war and for them, 31 October would always be Gheluvelt Day, the anniversary of the 2nd Battalion's glorious action in the First Battle of Ypres 1914. It not only saved Ypres and its salient from German occupation; it might even be said to have saved the entire British Expeditionary Force from being rolled up and crushed by the German military machine at the beginning of the First World War. The memorial in Gheluvelt village makes an even higher claim for the battle's ultimate significance:

> To the eternal memory of the officers and men of the 2nd Worcesters who on 31 October, fighting gloriously against a determined foe, gave their lives at Gheluvelt that civilisation might be saved.

By the end of October 1914, the British Army was fighting for its collective life, trying to hold off a fearsome German offensive intended to overwhelm that last part of Belgium as yet free from its philistine yoke. The German Army was resolved on taking Ypres, a critical road and rail hub, and then driving on to take the strategically important Channel ports of Ostend and Dunkirk. A withering barrage of artillery fire poured down on allied defenders of the salient around Ypres, a defensive line on the hills which formed the lip of a saucer encircling the city, lying on the shallow ground within it. Compounding the misery, the autumn rains flooded the scrapes, primitive trenches, which defenders hastily dug to provide cover from the ferocious bombardment. Only the sheer skill of experienced British infantrymen trained to fire rapidly and accurately (15 rounds a minute over 300 yards) ensured that the Germans took a severe toll and that the fragile defensive position held. Still, the British forces were outnumbered and outgunned; and weeks of intense fighting had exhausted men who had fought without relief or remission.

German attacks had focused late in the month on the north-east side of the salient, and the 2nd Worcesters had participated in the fighting there, at Langemarck, now the site of a brooding and atmospheric German cemetery. Only after a desperate but successful holding action, where they had been fighting shoulder-to-shoulder, were the Worcesters released, to allow them to retire for long-overdue recuperation at Halte (later known as Hellfire Corner) on the edge of Ypres itself. Corporal Jack Cole remembered that:

> Every man of the 2nd Worcesters was exhausted and unshaven and we were relieved to go back into reserve. But those days there was no such thing as rest! We'd only just arrived when the word came that we were urgently needed to stop another German attack, this time up the Ypres to Menin Road. We were absolutely fed up to the teeth.

So, the fatigued Worcesters were being transferred from one hot-spot on the salient to another, to Polygon Wood, south of Ypres. In the middle of the night they followed Major Hankey, their commanding officer, in single file down the Menin Road until they turned off left up into Polygon Wood where the Germans had made a breakthrough. The Worcesters were tasked with driving the enemy out of the wood and there, dodging between the trees and barely able to see in the dark, they found themselves in bitter hand-to-hand fighting. They went in with bayonets, Cole describing it in the language of boyhood death and glory tales:

> It was cold, remorseless steel; Major Hankey led us with sword in hand. The hordes of Germans were fresh-faced boys. But they were tough youngsters. We were unshaven, and we were haggard in comparison. But we went into them stabbing.

Another 2nd Worcester, Captain Stacke, later described how his men cheered in 'a pursuit (which) continued for over half a mile', but then how, 'as the wood began to thin and daylight showed between the trees, sharp bursts of fire from the edge of open ground brought the advance to a stop…and the battalion met a storm of shrapnel and machine-gun bullets'. At that point, with bodies strewn through the undergrowth, and piled in groups where the fighting had been heaviest, the two sides halted to solidify their positions: the Worcesters standing on a line around the wood supported by machine guns at each corner; the Germans digging into hastily scratched trenches just below the wood, too close for comfort.

Yet there was to be only a short, restless remission for the Worcesters; they were damp, bedraggled, and were forced to sleep in the open in the couple of days they had before their defining action. For the time being they were held in reserve. It would become clear soon enough that Polygon Wood had been secured only temporarily, for the German High Command was now planning to unleash what they fully expected to be the *coup de*

Mercian Regiment Museum (Worcestershire)

The 2nd Worcester Regiment at the Chateau Gheluvelt, 31 October 1914.

grâce. A new army – five additional infantry divisions, augmented by 260 heavy guns – was moving up the Menin Road determined to burst through to Ypres and beyond. German company commanders read out a special order of the day:

> The breakthrough will be of decisive importance. We must and will therefore conquer, settle for ever with the centuries long struggle, end the war and strike the decisive blow against our most detested enemy.

The language – both portentous and contemptuous – reflected the personal animus the Kaiser felt for the English. It was thus especially appropriate that he should arrive on the day of battle at Gheluwe, a mile east of Gheluvelt, to witness and to gloat at his mortal enemy's annihilation. And all the signs, as battle commenced at 6am on the morning of 31 October, were that his hopes would be swiftly realised. A devastating bombardment from the German heavy guns obliterated the village of Gheluvelt, to be followed by wave upon wave of advancing infantrymen; such was the weight of the assault that British gunners were forced to limber up and haul their guns back down the Menin Road towards Ypres, whilst riflemen from The Queen's and Scots Fusiliers, the Welch and the King's Royal Rifles fought themselves to a standstill. Just to the north-east of the ruined village, Gheluvelt Chateau was being staunchly defended by the decimated forces of the South Wales Borderers. All that prevented a speedy conclusion to the battle was a certain lack of resolution on the part of the Germans on the ground, who determined to mop up stubborn pockets of resistance prior to forging on down the road to Ypres.

However, there was one slim ray of light for the British in this allegorical darkness; a single telephone wire back to Headquarters remained intact to transmit a desperate appeal for help. Brigadier-General Charles FitzClarence there resolved on immediate action; he had no formal authority over a battalion belonging to a different division, but these were desperate straits. He later reflected that so intense was the German assault, this must constitute the last stand of the British Army in Belgium. He went to find Major Hankey at the edge of the battlefield. They spoke for twenty minutes as the brigadier outlined the situation. Asked what his men were like, Hankey replied that they were 'first rate, ready to do anything reasonable'. FitzClarence apocryphally retorted: "There's nothing reasonable about what I'm going to order them to do. The village must be retaken or the war's lost. You're all I've got left.'

Hankey's force of 370 men and eight officers gathered at the south-west corner of the wood, looking down across open fields to Gheluvelt, where the church tower alone was just visible above the smoke-wreathed village. He immediately deployed his battalion scouts to move ahead and cut any wire obstructing the passage down to the village. At 2pm – issued with extra ammunition, and with bayonets fixed – the Worcesters charged out of the wood, following Major Hankey down the open field under a hail of shrapnel from German artillery, which inflicted around one hundred casualties. In the tumult of battle all Hankey could remember was 'deafening noise; retreating men; shouting commands'. The attack took the Worcesters across a light railway line, through hedges and wire fences to the edge of parkland separated from the village by a tree-lined sunken road; that parkland gave onto the Chateau's gardens which surrounded the shuttered house and its precious statuary.

Such was the thick cloud enveloping the battlefield, the pace of the attack, the youth and inexperience of the German units and their preoccupation with the stubborn pocket of resistance presented by the South Wales Borderers, that Hankey and his men, bursting through the hedge bounding the lawns took the German infantry (some 1,000 or so) completely by surprise. Many of them had been enjoying the fruits of victory, exploring the Chateau and outhouses. The Worcesters joined the Borderers, who were at their last gasp, on the lawn: Hankey recognised an old friend commanding the Welshmen, Colonel Burleigh Leach, and exclaimed: 'God, fancy meeting you here!' 'Thank God you have come,' Leach responded. Meanwhile men from both battalions set about the Germans with bayonet and rifle-butt, routing them from the chateau, Jack Cole (again) reminiscing that:

> They fled in a solid grey mass and we watched our boys winkling them out. Remorseless. It was slaughter. At one point on the sunken road we were firing the machine guns with their bodies for cover. We linked up with the Welch and had to clear out Germans, sweeping the sunken road with enfilade fire. And we did it, apart from a few fanatics. We plugged the gap to Calais.

The Germans believed they had been attacked by a much larger force, which probably explains the ease with which the Worcesters could go on to clear Gheluvelt village itself after a house-to-house (or rather, ruin-to-ruin) search. Only a few Saxons held on to some scattered houses in the south-east of the village. The bulk of the enemy force had fled. By the evening, with the artillery dug in to new positions back up the Menin Road, and the German forces temporarily dislocated before regathering, the position had been stabilised.

And this is the importance of Gheluvelt. The Worcesters had stopped the German advance dead in its tracks. Perhaps no one knew better than the Commander-in-Chief himself, Sir John French, just how important was this action. Partly it was a matter of context. The Worcesters had gone into action at the very moment that he was receiving the shattering news that British High Command at Hooge had been wiped out by a single shell scoring a direct hit, and that the defences at Gheluvelt had been overwhelmed; he had little doubt 'that the last barrier between the Germans and the Channel seaboard was broken down'. He would later describe that lunchtime as 'the worst half hour of my life'. Yet within short order the 2nd Worcesters had shored up that crumbling line and provided precious time to regroup. Although that same evening FitzClarence would direct them to make an orderly retreat, to prepared and readily defensible positions at Veldhoek, back up the road to Ypres, this was the tipping point of the First Battle of Ypres. Indeed, Ypres and the Belgian ports would not now fall; in fact, they never did throughout the remaining four years of war. Quite as important as this military reality was the psychological effect of the Worcesters' action. French recovered his equilibrium and recognised that 'the 2nd Worcesters had behaved with the utmost

Ceremony to mark the opening of Gheluvelt Park in Worcester in 1922, a memorial to those lost during the Battle of Gheluvelt in 1914.

gallantry'. And fellow soldiers were invigorated by the victory. A gunner with the newly sited guns on the Menin Road, C. B. Burrows, wrote in his diary entry for 31 October how he heard, 'we done good and have repulsed their attack. Stay here all night and keep up a heavy rate of fire. Heard that enemy infantry were lying dead in heaps – also that we have lost heavy. Shall not forget this day in a hurry'.

Nor has Worcester forgotten that day in a hurry. On 17 June 1922 that same Field Marshal John French, now ennobled as 1st Earl of Ypres, came to Worcester to open Gheluvelt Park, created to commemorate the men who fought and died in a heroic action. French underlined its importance for the benefit of proud citizens attending the ceremony: 'On that day the 2nd Worcesters saved the British Empire,' he said. In 2010 a striking metal sculpture was unveiled in the Park. It has 27 panels, one for each two-month period in the war. The panels are of different heights, each centimetre representing 500 British and Commonwealth casualties. The involvement of the 2nd Worcesters is marked by a final panel inscribed with the names of all those men who made the ultimate sacrifice on that famous day at Gheluvelt on 31 October 1914.

CHAPTER 18
Woodbine Willie

Image produced by kind permission of Tudor House Museum from its Changing Face of Worcester collection- www.cfow.org.uk

Geoffrey Studdert Kennedy, 1883-1929,
army chaplain known as 'Woodbine Willie'.

A trench war of attrition lasting four long years followed the Battle of Gheluvelt on the Western Front. This Worcester moment is not about set-piece battles but rather about efforts to succour the soldiers spiritually in and out of battle. Central to this was the role of the 3,400 military padres – Anglican and other denominations – who by August 1918 ministered to Tommy Atkins. These padres divided opinion. Some soldiers saw them as too middle class, allied to the upper-class officers who sent them into battle, and as – all too often – steeling their resolve to fight, while making themselves scarce when the going got hot.

An example of this can be found in the autobiography of the author Frank Richards, who thought the chaplains 'a funny crowd: they prayed for victory and thundered for the enemy to be smitten hip and thigh, but did not believe in doing any of the smiting themselves'. However, this type of judgement seems unduly harsh and probably unrepresentative, bearing in mind that three-quarters of the recruits would have attended Sunday School as children, that a deeply ingrained spiritual sense ran through the soldiery, that most appear to have believed simply that there was a Higher Being before whom there would be an eventual reckoning, and that many testimonies relate the consolation to be found in the undemonstrative support of the best of the military chaplains, those who shared danger with them.

The importance of Worcester's own Woodbine Willie, the Reverend Geoffrey Studdert Kennedy, vicar of St Paul's, was that he represented all that was best in military chaplains; he won an enduring national reputation and along with Neville Talbot, the founder of Toc H, he was the most famous padre of the whole war. His upbringing and early years as a priest ensured that his ministry was rooted in the lives of ordinary working men and it was that familiarity that made him so effective when transposed to the front line in the heat of battle. Born in 1883 not in Worcester but in Leeds, the son of a vicar whose benefice was in the poorest part of the city, there was also a strain of Irishness in him which – he always said – explained his 'gift of the gab'. The grimy slums around St Mary's Quarry Hill – and their impoverished inhabitants – had a lasting impact on Studdert Kennedy, for he was to spend his whole life helping the poor, giving it political expression by his adoption of the tenets of Christian Socialism.

He was well – and happily – educated at Leeds Grammar School and then Trinity College, Dublin where he took a First in Classics and Divinity. But even if his academic credentials suggested he would become a high-flyer in whatever profession he chose, he determined instead – after a spell training at Rugby Clergy College – to serve the poorest areas of industrial England. First, he worked as a deacon attached to Rugby parish church, ministering to tramps, to those dwelling in lodging houses and those frequenting the pubs in the town's slum areas. After spells running the town's mission and then helping his father back in Leeds, he was asked to become vicar of St Paul's in Worcester in June 1914. It had, in Studdert Kennedy's words, 'the smallest income and the poorest people' (*c.* 4,000 of them), and the church itself was surrounded by back-to-back houses with shared sanitation facilities, one toilet and washhouse to twelve houses. Yet, as was often the case, an Anglo-Catholic church, with its ritual, colour, and mild exoticism, had a real appeal to working-class parishioners. Reinforcing that was the work of the priest himself; for Studdert Kennedy was no ordinary middle-class cleric, and through his impulsive generosity, a conviction that he must act to do good, not simply mouth platitudes, 'a large number of his parishioners owed their stability, position and hope to his wise and timely help' (in the words of Dean Moore Ede). He gave so freely – even food and furniture as well as hospitality – that he and his family would go short at times; he also gave of his time, preaching in the streets, chatting to men in the pubs, organising outdoor services. Yet, no sooner had he started to establish himself in Worcester than war broke out on the Continent; as for all others of his generation it would transform him.

At the beginning, he had echoed the sentiments of many other clergymen – that, in the words of Bishop Winnington-Ingram, this war was 'a great crusade, to kill Germans to save the world…to kill them lest the civilisation of the world should itself be killed'. When he made a call to arms in early autumn 1914 in Worcester his words were conventional: 'I cannot say too strongly that I believe every able-bodied man ought to volunteer for service anywhere. There must be no shirking of duty'. These bullish attitudes did not long survive his first encounters with the reality of war, when he joined up in December 1915. He had been itching to enlist but soon enough he would share the disillusionment of other army chaplains who had started out with noble ideals about a glorious and just war, men like the Reverend Charles Doudney who wrote despairingly: 'The flowers are long gone, and their perfume is replaced by the all-pervading stench of putrefaction fraught with chloride of lime; it's the smell of the charnel-house, and in places is added the strange effluvium, indescribable, of newly-shed blood.' And men like the Catholic priest, Father Francis Drinkwater who wrote in the aftermath to the first day of the Somme: 'I shall soon be a pacifist and conscientious objector. It becomes more impossible every month, and the ghastly mangling of human beings en masse seems disproportionate to any conceivable object.'

Studdert Kennedy rapidly came to regret his initial reaction to war and instead lamented that 'the brutality of war is unutterable', writing in one of his poems – for like so many other combatants, poetry was the most convenient and immediate vehicle for conveying the profound emotions stirred by the conflict –

> Waste of Blood, waste of tears
> Waste of youth's most precious years.

He went on to reflect – self-deprecatingly – on his role as padre:

> What the bloody hell is the Church doing here? An amateur stretcher-bearer or an amateur undertaker? Was that all a Christian priest could be in this ruin of a rotten civilisation? I have pondered as I sat down after singing a comic song to the men at rest. An amateur comedian struggling to make men forget for one short hour the horrors in the midst of which they live and

are called upon to die; always an amateur, always more or less inefficient and untrained.

This *cri de coeur* distills some of the essence of what being a chaplain came to mean for Studdert Kennedy. He found his purpose within hours of arriving in France, at the Rouen staging post, where troops in their hundreds got off the trains to stretch their legs for a few hours, before continuing their journey up to the Front. He mixed with the men, intent on raising their spirits; he sang songs to – and with – them, he would deliver a comforting Christian message in a few short words, and – as the men boarded the trains he would walk up and down the trains offering two different comforts to them – from one haversack he withdrew Woodbine cigarettes and from the other copies of the New Testament.

He was deeply affected by the emotion and the sense of impending doom in these Rouen departures:

> There is nothing glorious about the departure. It is all sordid and filthy. God only knows the hardships endured on these journeys in packed and dirty carriages. No place to wash, no place to move, they sit and wait for eighteen hours or more.

Once posted from Rouen to the front line, Studdert Kennedy recognised that the best way to be useful was to share the lives of the soldiers: unlike the chaplains Frank Richards cited, he joined in the training at the infantry camp and he went into battle with them. He was able to communicate with them because he didn't hesitate to swear as colourfully as they did. Equally he recognised that it was inappropriate to evangelise too enthusiastically in the heightened tension of the front line. He gave advice to a new chaplain about his work:

> He asked me about purely spiritual works. I said there is very little: it is all muddled and mixed. Live with the men, go where they go, make up your mind to share all their risks and more if you can do any good. You can take it that the best place for a padre to be is where there is the most danger of death. Our first job is to go beyond the men in self-sacrifice and reckless devotion. Take a box of fags in your haversack and a great deal of love in your heart and go up to them. Laugh with them, joke with them. You can pray with them sometimes but pray for them always.

That 'box of fags' came to be Studdert Kennedy's trademark, and back home in Worcester townspeople generously responded; shop-keepers placed boxes on their shop-counters collecting money for his Woodbines to distribute to the men, and when home on leave, Studdert Kennedy toured the shops personally to thank them. But his fame was not just prescribed by the dispensing of cigarettes. As the advice cited above makes clear, reckless courage won men's respect and affection and made his mission easier; in June 1917 at Messines Ridge that selfless bravery was

Huge crowds turned out for Woodbine Willie's funeral in Worcester, 1929.

rewarded with a Military Cross. Morphine supplies had run out at a dressing station and he volunteered to fetch more from another station. He dashed over open ground under heavy bombardment, sprinting from shell-hole to shell-hole, and as he went (in the citation in the *London Gazette*) he 'searched shell-holes for our own and enemy wounded; his cheerful endurance had a splendid effect upon all ranks'. He self-deprecatingly described what prompted him:

> An advanced collecting post for wounded in the Ypres Salient. A boy with a badly shattered thigh in a corner moaning and yelling by turns for 'Somefing to stop the pain.' (But) there was no morphia. That was the horror. Someone must go for it. I went. I went because the hell outside was less awful than the hell in. I didn't go to do a heroic deed or perform a Christian service; I went because I couldn't bear that moaning any longer. I ran, and as I ran, and cowered down in the shell-holes, I thought…If I get through and bring the morphia back, it will be like bringing back heaven to him…I will be to him a saviour from hell. I'd like that…

Predictably, as British lines buckled under the ferocious onslaught of the Ludendorff offensive in March 1918, military authorities looked for leaders who could inspire men whose morale was badly dented; they insisted he speak to troops on all parts of the Front because – in the words of Dean Moore Ede of Worcester again – 'of his wonderful power of reviving courage and of inspiring men'. Unlike some chaplains, he had walked the walk himself; when he called for resolute defiance the men knew he was all too aware of what that meant in reality. Great personal courage; invigorating preaching; a rare talent for communicating with men at their level, in their own language: all these attributes conspired to give Woodbine Willie national fame by the war's end in 1918. It helped that George V himself took a shine to him; Studdert Kennedy preached at Buckingham Palace and was appointed a Royal chaplain.

The Armistice allowed him to return to St Paul's and to take up the reins both of family life, and of his mission to the poor in his parish. He was now a well-recognised and much-admired Worcester figure, with a national profile. That celebrity led him to resign from St Paul's in 1921, although he continued to live on the Bromyard Road in the city until his death. Increasingly he had found that invitations to preach all over the country, as well as his greater activism in the Christian Socialist movement, distracted him from his pastoral work in his parish. His disenchantment with post-war Britain radicalised him and drew him into national campaigning for a visionary new approach to politics. The working-men alongside whom he had fought had been promised they would return to a 'Land fit for Heroes'. Studdert Kennedy's response to the grinding poverty, housing crisis and the rising joblessness in the early 1920s was to organise a protest march of 800 Worcester unemployed from Pitchcroft to the Guildhall to raise awareness of their plight.

To the end, then, Geoffrey Studdert Kennedy remained utterly consistent in this regard: he saw his mission as reaching out to the poorest people in industrial Britain. His role was to improve their spiritual, and their physical, lives. His work in Worcester was given a deeper resonance when translated to the Western Front, where he became one of the leading military chaplains in the conflict, respected both by troops and by High Command. Fame did not turn his head; he did not become an establishment figure. In a very real sense, despite his country-wide profile after 1918, he never left Worcester, and the city's regard for their famous pastor was evident in 1929 when tragically young (he was 46) he died of complications arising from asthma, 'flu and pneumonia. Worcester's streets were lined for the passing of his coffin, and people filed past it in their hundreds when it came to rest in St Paul's church prior to his funeral.

CHAPTER 19

Worcester at War 1939–1945

Worcester is far from the Channel coast and from London which were in the vanguard of engagement with Hitler; and yet its proximity to Birmingham and Coventry, those vital centres of armaments and military supplies, meant that it too was more than peripheral to the war effort. Indeed, as we shall see, it had a very particular role to play in plans to thwart invasion. Malcolm Atkin, the former County Archaeologist, has written: 'It had always been assumed Worcester would have been a backwater during an invasion. Actually, it was on the frontline'.

In one sense that last statement is seemingly contradicted by the plans at the very outset in September 1939 which made of Worcester a refuge for government, key civil servants and even the Royal Family. As a result, we have the curious sight of the King's School boarders being evacuated to two hotels in Criccieth on the north side of Cardigan Bay (while the Grammar School hosted the day boys), and of Malvern College boys setting up school in Blenheim Palace; in both cases their buildings were required by the authorities: Malvern's Science Block commandeered for the Admiralty as the central signal station for the British battle fleet, and the King's School to serve for staff of the Air Ministry. King's returned within a year.

Worcestershire, then, was deemed safe enough from enemy attention to host operations which were under threat in London. Even as Neville Chamberlain was delivering his ultimatum to Hitler, with invasion of Poland imminent, unmarked lorries were bearing cases of food supplies to the capacious cellars of Madresfield Court just outside Worcester. The moated stately home was earmarked for the Royal Family to be a staging post before flight to Wales and passage to Canada and the New World to escape Nazi clutches. There are echoes here of a national emergency a century earlier. Then in November 1803 King George III wrote to the Bishop of Worcester: 'We are here in daily expectation that Bonaparte will attempt his threatened invasion. Should his troops effect a landing… I shall think it right the queen and my daughters should cross the Severn, and shall send them to your episcopal palace at Worcester.'

His Majesty's government was destined for Hindlip Hall in Worcester, once a centre of Catholic intrigue (see Chapter 8), while Winston Churchill and his staff were to operate from Spetchley Park, on the south-eastern outskirts, where Oliver Cromwell had prepared his winning strategy for the Battle of Worcester in 1651 (see Chapter 11). New buildings to house 16,000 key staff were hastily erected on Whittington Road and Comer Road, Worcester. Transmission of the code words 'Black Move' would have signalled this evacuation from London; in May/June 1940 it must have seemed an imminent possibility as France and the Low

Bomb damage in Worcester, 1942.

Countries were overrun by the German war machine and Hitler's forces contemplated invasion twenty miles away.

Others did move to Worcester and the surrounding area for comparative safety, like Queen Wilhelmina of the Netherlands who briefly made Croome Court her home, and the Belgian Army which made its HQ at the Abbey Hotel, Malvern for a rather longer stay. Malvern, just eight miles from Worcester, was indeed a veritable hub for Free Europe with its high-ranking Polish naval officers, Free French cadets, some 500 Dutch soldiers and airmen, invalided GIs and French Canadians. Nor was the area simply a human refuge; the Telecommunications Research Establishment (TRE) moved from Swanage in Dorset to Malvern to develop radar in ways absolutely vital to winning the war: AI (aerial interception) allowed allied night fighters to use radar technology to engage the enemy, ASV (air to surface radar) enabled British planes to locate and destroy U-boats in the Battle of the Atlantic, and radar-jamming did a great deal to frustrate the German use of radar. One aviation historian has written: 'Without doubt the War's outcome was influenced by TRE's H2S radar enabling Bomber Command to locate its targets and giving Coastal Command the means to seek and destroy the enemy in the North Atlantic.'

Much of the practical work was carried out at neighbouring RAF Defford, a few miles south-west of Worcester; it was the main station in Britain for the development of radar. RAF Comberton a few miles away was one of five inland radar stations in Britain tasked with detecting, locating and tracking enemy aircraft as they approached the country.

Worcester's contribution to the country's war effort took a number of forms. Other RAF stations – Pershore and Honeybourne – hosted bombers while her soldiers in the Worcestershire Regiment fought in all the main theatres of the war. The 1st Battalion saw service in East Africa before defeat at the hands of Rommel at Tobruk; the 2nd Battalion fought in Burma and assisted in the victory at Mandalay, while the Territorials in their different battalions were involved at Dunkirk, at Kohima and Imphal in Burma, and in Operation Epsom in the Normandy campaign in July 1944. Worcestershire's civilians would have had a sharp reminder about the human cost of war as traumatised survivors from the British Expeditionary Force at Dunkirk recuperated in the makeshift camp on the meadows at Evesham in the summer of 1940. Their response was probably less sympathetic when they encountered the German POWs corralled at Honeybourne and Hampton Lovett.

Quite as important as military engagement was the contribution to propaganda and to the secret war made by BBC Wood Norton and BBC Droitwich, just miles outside Worcester. Wood Norton's staff specialised in monitoring enemy broadcasts; Droitwich hosted the BBC European Service which broadcast allied news and editorials, as well as the Voice of America and additionally – and most importantly – transmitted coded prearranged messages to the Resistance in Occupied Europe, summoning cells to sabotage or to help secret missions.

Central to Worcester's war effort was its industrial contribution. Like so much of the West Midlands it was involved in the national drive to produce armaments. The output of surge drums for barrage balloons and of mining equipment from *MECO* the Mining and Engineering Company on Bromyard Road was evidently considered important enough to merit a targeted raid by a Junkers Ju88 bomber in October 1940 which killed seven and injured fifty others. Worcester's firms switched from consumer goods to arms and ammunition; rather uncharacteristically one might suppose, *Cadbury*, the Quaker chocolate firm – whose founder George Cadbury and whose widow Dame Elizabeth Cadbury had been such disciples of the Peace Movement – gave over its canal-side works at Diglis to producing ammunition for the Royal Ordnance, just as Kidderminster's famous carpet factories also switched to making ammunition. *Lea and Perrins* manufactured surgical dressings alongside its famous sauce. It was less of a change for *Stewarts and Lloyds* of Halesowen, who increased the scale of their tube-making to manufacture sections of PLUTO, the huge underwater oil pipeline which ran from Britain to France to supply the D-Day forces in 1944. Furthermore, the city hosted key storage facilities, with general fuel and oil supplies housed at Diglis docks, while the Odeon cinema in the centre of the city was requisitioned to store parts for Spitfires.

Worcester was only a southern outlier for the great Birmingham armaments industry in which former car factories manufactured Spitfires, Beaufighters, other aeroplanes and aero engines and aircraft components as well as military vehicles. *Dunlop* made the tyres for those self-same trucks and lorries, while from BSA there issued forth a flood of arms and guns as well as motorbikes. This explains why, from early in the War, Worcester was being prepared for a very special strategic role. It was earmarked as a centre of resistance to allow the British Army to fall back behind it and regroup if the invasion came. It would protect the country's key industrial production centres to its north and would guard against attack from the west, up the Bristol Channel and from Ireland, which was thought to be unreliable. A stop-line of defences ringing Worcester along the Teme, Severn, Avon rivers and the Oxford canal was to be created which, in the words of the Western Command instruction issued on 5 July 1940 (in the darkest hours when invasion seemed a realistic prospect):

> would extend through all vulnerable parts a number of lines in which the enemy advancing with tanks from the east and west will find no gaps or weak places.

The line would be reinforced at key points with road and rail blocks, with defence posts at crossing-points and with barriers to obstruct potential landing grounds from any German airborne assault. Behind it, Worcester (along with Kidderminster and Redditch), would have been turned into a tank-trap to hold up the inevitable German advance once that line of resistance had been broken. These anti-tank trap islands would lure German armour into a nodal point where tanks were vulnerable to attack from above. Worcester had a 'keep', a central strong-point based on the Cross and the shopping centre, manned by men from the Home Guard 1st Battalion, directed from a Headquarters based on the Royal Grammar School buildings in the Tything. Had the situation demanded, many of the city's half-timbered houses and historic buildings would have been bull-dozed to create the tank-trap.

Nor was that the end of these defence preparations. The efforts of local archaeologists have unearthed the dozens of surviving pill boxes, glider traps and other fortifications in the fields ringing the south of Worcester; nearly all face westwards, a clear indication that an attack from the Bristol Channel and from Wales was anticipated. More than this, further evidence has emerged of a secret resistance army of farmers, teenage boy scouts and estate workers. Herefordshire and Worcestershire formed the most inland elements of the GHQ Auxiliary Units recruited during the summer of 1940 to carry out sabotage and resist an enemy invasion force. The Operational Base of Worcester's GHQ was Speyd's Coppice on the north side of the A44 between Cotheridge and Broadwas on Worcester's west side. This would have

Crown copyright, courtesy of DAHG & National Trust

Flight Telecommunications Flying Unit in front of a Lancaster bomber, RAF Defford 1946.

coordinated the secret army, which prepared itself by digging secret bunkers and stocking with food, ammunition and explosives. They were trained in secret, Home Guard uniforms serving as cover for inquisitive family members. They were organised into eight patrols. Their nocturnal sabotage would target fuel stores, ammunition dumps, the main railway lines focusing on Worcester, tank laagers and lorry parks.

Were the invasion to be successful they would go into hiding and emerge at night to harass enemy lines. There was one additional element to these secret preparations; evidence has emerged of a spy-ring centred on Upton-upon-Severn, eight miles from Worcester. It recruited vicars, doctors and vets – reputable, professional sorts who would have a good reason to travel – apparently innocently – about occupied Worcestershire. They were tasked to note troop movements, details of the regimental insignia, and the strength of German units in occupation of the area; as in any lurid spy fiction tale, they were trained to make their notes on edible rice paper to confound the enemy.

The invasion, of course, did not happen and by 1941 Adolf Hitler had concentrated his attention on the East, which was to prove his nemesis. After 1940 many of these young recruits subsequently joined the regular forces and the spies continued with their daily round. The government and Royal Family stayed put in London to stiffen public morale during the Blitz. Worcester reverted to its largely unhindered contribution to arms production. But for a brief moment the city had been envisaged as the nation's last redoubt, scene of the last heroic stand against an invading army in what would then have been a largely hopeless cause.

CHAPTER 20

Worcestershire County Cricket Club, Basil D'Oliveira and Apartheid

Few cricket grounds in the world can rival New Road in Worcester for the beauty and grandeur of its setting, with the Cathedral and College Hall providing a medieval backdrop on the far side of the Severn. It is a quintessentially English scene; for international cricket sides starting their tour, the experience of that first match at Worcester, played on emerald green sward in early May, would constitute an imperishable memory. By the 1960s those tourists would also be struck by the strength of the opposition for, after sixty relatively undistinguished years in the County Championship, Worcestershire had become a serious force, winning successive titles in 1964 and 1965, through the efforts of a clutch of Test players, amongst whom Tom Graveney was the acknowledged star.

That 1965 triumph was notable, too, for the meteoric emergence of a man whose struggles to express his exceptional talent in the 1960s would provoke international controversy, and place Worcestershire County Cricket Club at the very centre of a political and sporting conflict. This was Basil D'Oliveira, the Cape Coloured – mixed race – South African whose serendipitous journey to a Test cricket career denied him in his native South Africa, took him first to the Lancashire League and then, through the good auspices of Tom Graveney, to sign for Worcestershire.

In the best senses of the word, life firstly in Middleton (Lancashire) and then in Worcester, was an education for D'Oliveira. Colour was no bar to entry in hotels and public amenities, and he was treated with courtesy, respect and indeed affection. Where back in South Africa he had been forced to play on wasteland, joining team mates to clear the makeshift ground of stones and then to carry, roll out and peg down the matting wicket, in Worcester the impeccably curated turf was a shock. In Cape Town, such facilities were the jealously guarded perquisites of the white minority. They were the physical manifestation of a prevailing apartheid policy founded on the idea of the separation of races. And it was an article of apartheid faith that racially inferior blacks and coloureds did not have the same aptitude for cricket as whites; facilities like Newlands, the cathedral of South African sport, would have been wasted on them.

In truth Basil D'Oliveira, born in 1931 and growing up on Signal Point, Cape Town, was only the most gifted of a number of coloured South Africans who surmounted adversity to become formidable cricketers, as the Kenya national team discovered in the late 1950s when a Non-White South African team captained by Basil D'Oliveira put them to the sword. The uneven and erratic matting pitches developed in D'Oliveira – and his team-mates – a watchful technique which later stood him in good stead in the test arena. These disadvantaged black and coloured Cape Town clubs nevertheless insisted on the highest standards of dress in their players – clean boots, club ties, blazers – and of behaviour (including 'walking', not waiting for the umpire to give one out). Lewis D'Oliveira, Basil's influential and strong-minded father, was just such a martinet in his insistence on these fundamentals. As Peter Oborne puts it in his seminal book, *Basil D'Oliveira, Cricket and Conspiracy: The Untold Story*: 'Players sensed that fair play did not exist in the society in which they lived – so created a version of it on the cricket field'.

In more than a decade of brilliant performances with bat and ball, including a memorable innings of 225 in just 70 minutes, Basil D'Oliveira had established himself as a unique talent in non-white South African cricket; only the iniquity of apartheid prevented him from proving himself among a generation of outstanding white cricketers like Graeme and Peter Pollock and Barry Richards. So, he looked abroad, to England, and by great good fortune, and discerning judgement, he alighted on the legendary broadcaster John Arlott, whose commentaries, delivered in a ripe Hampshire burr, seemed the incarnation of cricket and its enduring values. Perhaps D'Oliveira knew – or intuited – that Arlott loathed apartheid, having seen for himself the brutal treatment of a black African when on a tour in the 1940s. D'Oliveira's frequent letters to him, and his own researches, led Arlott to arrange for D'Oliveira to come to England as a Lancashire League professional. How could he afford to travel? The extraordinary fund-raising of the coloured communities to pay for D'Oliveira's flight illustrates the extent to which he was their totem and their hope. His every innings would be followed hungrily.

By the time the 1960 English season got underway he was in his late 20s, and although he took time to settle he spent two years watching English players and studying English conditions. He developed a durable playing philosophy, based on the premise that the first hour of every innings should be given to the bowler, and only after he had played himself in would he allow himself the freedom to open up. It stood him in excellent stead at Worcester and in international matches.

Success at Middleton, where he established himself as the leading Lancashire League performer, led to that conversation with Tom Graveney, who had seen for himself

Patrick Eagar/Popperfoto/Getty Images

Basil D'Oliveira bats for Worcestershire against Leicestershire in the Gillette Cup quarter-final, 1973.

D'Oliveira's destructive power on a tour to Nkana (Northern Rhodesia). Worcestershire were fortunate that Lancashire failed to grab him – there is an early hint of ignorant prejudice in Lancashire's omission. But in Worcester D'Oliveira found nothing but whole-hearted support. He rewarded it with championship-winning performances in 1965, when the county followed up on its 1964 title. His very first match yielded a century, in cold, overcast conditions ideal for Essex's skilful seam attack; so did his second. At the end of the season he had made five centuries, bowled tightly and penetratively, and *Wisden* concluded that 'few newcomers can have made such an impression in their opening season as did Basil D'Oliveira'. But he was an old man in a hurry – he was now 33 years old, even if he admitted to being only 30. If he were to play Test cricket he needed to make an immediate mark.

In 1966, in addition to scoring over 1,200 runs for Worcestershire, he was selected to play for England against the West Indies, an outstanding team and an especially fearsome prospect with the intimidating fast-bowling of

Wes Hall and Charlie Griffith. D'Oliveira survived, where a number of English batsmen wilted; more than that he flourished, so that the doyen of cricketing writers, C.L.R. James, could aver that 'D'Oliveira had destroyed the myth of the unplayability of West Indian fast-bowling'. Wes Hall had never before or since been hit for a straight six like that executed by D'Oliveira. Just as importantly, D'Oliveira exposed how utterly risible was apartheid's presumption of innate coloured sporting inferiority. He was a potent symbol for non-white South Africans who followed his career closely; beyond that, his rapid advance to Test cricket won him a host of supporters in England. As Oborne puts it: 'There was something about Basil D'Oliveira and the obstacles he overcame that touched them beyond words…for (his story) was a parable of sheer guts, bloody-minded resilience and …sheer human goodness'. Worcester took to 'Dolly' or 'Bas' as its own; and Basil and his wife Naomi made the city their home, while Damian his son, and later Brett his grandson, would cement the family's loyalty and affection by playing with distinction for the county, in front of the New Road stand named after Basil D'Oliveira.

After a successful summer of Test cricket in 1967 against Pakistan and India, life for D'Oliveira became much more complicated. He was now determined to be selected for the MCC tour of South Africa scheduled for the winter of 1968/9; he would make history as the first coloured man to play in a Test match in South Africa, and he wanted to experience both the passionate enthusiasm of those coloured people caged in their separate enclosure at Newlands, and the hostility of condescending white supremacists. Prime Minister Johannes Vorster and his ruling party now planned seriously for the eventuality; an incautious Minister P.M.K. Le Roux admitted that 'our policy is clear that we will not allow mixed teams to play against our white teams here', but Vorster did not want that policy to be stated as baldly and explicitly, preferring to avoid an open confrontation which could lead to the severing of sporting links between South Africa and the home countries.

Firstly, he had cause to hope that D'Oliveira might not be selected at all. He had an undistinguished winter tour of the West Indies in 1967/8, losing form, and embracing the party scene too enthusiastically. And then, after he played (well) in a losing cause against the 1968 Australian tourists in the first Test of the summer, he was unaccountably dropped. Some sensed the duplicity of influential MCC committee men who were by now aware – through back channels – that the selection of D'Oliveira would force Vorster to block the tour. Much more convenient if D'Oliveira was not chosen at all. In Oborne's words: 'There was no need to sacrifice everything over some high-minded confrontation about an abstract principle'. At the Lords Test that summer senior South African cricket officials worked on MCC counterparts, part of Vorster's

Ken Kelly/Popperfoto/Getty Images

Celebrating his appointment as coach to Worcestershire County Cricket Club, 1979.

master-plan to ensure D'Oliveira was not selected for the South African tour.

Sadly, there was 'a depressing identity of interest, prejudice and approach between white South Africa and the British establishment.' Many in that self-same establishment wished to maintain cricketing links, either because a few sympathised with the racial outlook of South Africans, or because they did not want to look too closely at the reality of apartheid (for politics should not interfere with cricket), or because they argued disingenuously that maintaining contacts was the best hope for gradual change. Those contacts had signally failed up to 1968 to effect reform. At least the British Government in the shape of the Minister of Sport, Denis Howell, was unequivocal: he informed the Commons 'that the team to tour South Africa will be chosen on merit; any preconditions that the host country lays down will be totally disregarded'.

Influential MCC members like Lord Home and Lord Cobham tried to avoid any impulsive selection which would force Vorster's hand; and Cobham colluded with the secretary of the MCC, Billy Griffith, to try to persuade D'Oliveira to make himself unavailable for the tour. Throughout that summer they were aware that an apparently independent well-wisher, Tienie Oosthuizen, a rich businessman from South Africa (in truth operating at Vorster's behest), was offering D'Oliveira an exceedingly generous coaching contract (400% more than the going rate) to work with coloured cricketers in South Africa. The more D'Oliveira havered, in hopes of a recall to the English side and of another chance to pitch for a place on the tour, the more desperate and pressing was Oosthuizen with his bribe.

D'Oliveira was sorely tempted; but fate intervened. He was recalled for the last Ashes Test; with the series lost the selectors opted for change. It was a last chance to establish his claims; and he took it spectacularly. After a scratchy start, and an overnight break, he went on to hit a wonderful 158. If English supporters cheered a magnificent innings, many MCC committee members dreaded its consequences, while in South Africa Vorster believed it a calamity. Oborne argues: 'No other cricket innings has changed history. This one did. No other innings in Test history, to put the matter simply, has done anything like so much good'. He is surely correct, for the D'Oliveira affair would set in motion a chain reaction, in time leading to the isolation of South African cricket. This, with a wider sporting isolation, would do much in the next two decades to bring down an evil regime predicated on the separation and subjugation of races.

The selection meeting straight after D'Oliveira's grandstand performance in the Oval Test precipitated the crisis. He was omitted from the tour party. There were reasoned arguments as to why other batsmen were preferred, but the suspicion remains that some selectors made their decision to guarantee a tour took place. Perhaps most disappointing were those like Colin Cowdrey who promised D'Oliveira their support, and then in the committee room advocated his exclusion.

Basil D'Oliveira had driven home to Worcester, buoyed up after his Oval heroics, and was playing for the county against Sussex, scoring a century; he was in the dressing room at close of play when the shattering news came through that he had not been selected and, for once, a cocktail of emotions - hope, expectation, exhilaration and deep disappointment - overwhelmed him, and he broke down and wept. His old friend Tom Graveney got him home to bed, and after a brief interlude of profound despair he regained his equilibrium.

It was a testimony to his fundamental decency that there were later no recriminations; he was not sorry for himself; he did not rail against the selectors. He went on with his day job, scoring 402 runs in five innings after his shock exclusion. Oborne argued that D'Oliveira's own moderation, grace and gentility 'played a large part in educating the British people about the ugliness of apartheid'. Friends and Worcestershire supporters provided the balm of loyal affection for him and his family. Others did the protesting for him. Thousands of letters poured in to the County Ground and to his Worcester home. Some MCC members resigned and instigated a rebellion, which would be led by the cricketing Bishop of Woolwich, David Sheppard. Cricket writers attacked the MCC's selectors, E.W. Swanton exposing the hopeless illogicality of their argument that 'this cricketer who learned the game under the shadow of Table Mountain is essentially a man for English conditions'. John Arlott placed the affair in a wider context. 'This will prove far more than a sporting matter,' he opined. 'It could have such repercussions on British relations with the coloured races that the cancellation of a cricket tour would seem a trifling matter compared with British acceptance of Apartheid'. Arlott was percipient about the immense cricketing potential of Britain's Commonwealth immigrants if only they could be encouraged.

In the event the MCC committee found a way out. A vacancy on the tour party occurred through the injury to Tom Cartwright, the Warwickshire bowler; D'Oliveira was speedily added to the party, even though he was not a like-for-like replacement. He had only a brief moment of quiet satisfaction. Vorster meanwhile faced the unpalatable truth that all his plotting had come to nought. He furiously denounced the MCC for surrendering to a campaign of anti-apartheid leftists, and called off the tour, plunging South African cricket into lengthy quarantine.

D'Oliveira's test career continued into the 1970s; and he was a dominant presence in the Worcestershire team, playing a crucial role in another championship-winning generation in 1974. At the age of 46 he was still topping the county's batting averages, scoring 1,173 runs in a season. He did not retire from the fray until he was 48 in 1979, but he promptly went on to coach the county, developing a new young side which won the championship in successive years in 1988/9. From his debut in 1964 to his death in 2011 he would be the incarnation of Worcestershire's cricketing spirit and the Basil D'Oliveira stand at the New Road County Ground memorialises his outstanding contribution. Equally, he would be revered in Mandela's new multi-racial South Africa; for thousands of non-white South Africans he represented hope and defiance, while the D'Oliveira Affair exposed to the world the cruelties and evils of the apartheid regime.

Timeline

626–655	Penda rules Mercia, extending his rule into the Severn Valley
680	Archbishop Theodore founds the see of Worcester
884–899	Worcester fortified as a *burh* by Aethelred and Aethelflaeda to resist the Vikings
960	Dunstan briefly Bishop of Worcester before Oswald succeeds him in 961
983	Oswald's new Cathedral at Worcester completed
1041	Worcester becomes a centre of resistance to Harthacnut's taxes; Bevere Island on the Severn besieged by the king's vengeful forces
1062	Wulstan consecrated Bishop of Worcester
1066	The Norman Conquest
1088	Violent uprising against the king centred on Worcester but Wulstan holds firm for the king
1089	Wulstan's Cathedral completed
1095	Wulstan dies
1199	John succeeds Richard the Lionheart as King of England
1204	Normandy and most of the Angevin Empire lost to Philip Augustus
1208	England placed under an Interdict by Pope Innocent III
1215	Magna Carta; much of Eastern England, including London, is in rebel hands
1216	John dies; he requests burial in Worcester
1218	Boy king Henry III makes peace with Llewellyn at the Treaty of Worcester
1337–1453	The Hundred Years War against France
1455–1483	The Wars of the Roses between the Houses of York and Lancaster
1485	The Battle of Bosworth Field sees Henry Tudor defeat and kill Richard III
1486	Birth of Prince Arthur to Henry VII and Elizabeth of York
1492	Christopher Columbus discovers the New World
1500–1570s	Peak of Worcester's broadcloth industry
1501	Marriage of Arthur, Prince of Wales, to Katherine of Aragon
1502	Arthur dies at Ludlow, and is buried with due ceremony in Worcester
1509	Henry VIII, Arthur's younger brother, succeeds to the throne
1517	Martin Luther publishes his 95 Theses in Wittenberg to initiate the Protestant Reformation
1533	Impatient for an heir, Henry divorces Catherine of Aragon and marries Anne Boleyn
1534	Parliament passes the Act of Supremacy, making the King the Supreme Head of the English Church
1535	Hugh Latimer made Bishop of Worcester
1535-6	Smaller religious houses closed after a national Visitation; Thomas Cromwell is the architect of the strategy
1536	The Pilgrimage of Grace

Timeline

1536-40 Larger monasteries dissolved

1539 Worcester Priory dissolved

1541 Foundation of the King's Schools, one of which is created in Worcester

1547 Henry VIII dies; succeeded by Edward VI

1553-58 Reign of Mary I who restored Catholicism

1555 Latimer – along with Ridley – burnt at the stake in Oxford for their Protestant beliefs

1558 Elizabeth I accedes to the throne

1575 Elizabeth I's visit to Worcester

1590 Royal Charter establishes Worcester's Clothiers' Guild

1596 Thomas Tomkins becomes organist and master of the choristers at Worcester

1603 James VI of Scotland becomes James I of England, the first Stuart king

1605 Gunpowder Plot; Catholic Worcestershire suffers retribution

1620 Edward Winslow crosses the Atlantic in the *Mayflower* as a Pilgrim Father

1622 Tomkins publishes his *Songs of 3.4.5. and 6. Parts* – madrigal masterpieces

1640 Long Parliament and increasingly acrimonious relations between the King and many gentry represented there

1642 First hostilities in the First Civil War take place at Powick on Worcester's southern edge. Parliament occupies Worcester after Royalist retreat; in turn Parliament abandons the city in autumn 1642 until …

1646 Worcester's siege and surrender to Parliament; Cathedral closed up

1649 Charles I executed; Tomkins the Royalist writes *Sad Pavan: for these distracted times*

1651 The Battle of Worcester sees Charles II beaten by Oliver Cromwell; he flees the country

1656 Tomkins dies in 'exile' at Martin Hussingtree

1660 Restoration of Charles II

1685 The openly Catholic James II succeeds his brother

1687 James II visits Worcester and attends a Catholic chapel in the Tything.
In Oxford he insists Magdalen College's Fellows appoint a Catholic President instead of John Hough who was later translated to the bishopric at Worcester

1688 John Somers of Worcester leads for the defence in the trial of the Seven Bishops who had resisted the royal prerogative; he secured their freedom

James II flees the country and William III and his wife Mary are invited in from Holland to be constitutional monarchs

1689 Somers would shape the Glorious Revolution in the Bill of Rights

William III leads Britain into the Nine Years War against Louis XIV of France

1697 As Baron Somers of Evesham, appointed Lord Chancellor

1701-13 War of the Spanish Succession; Britain fights to stop Louis XIV dominating the Continent

1702 William III dieds; Anne succeeds him

1714 George I, the first Hanoverian king, succeeds Anne

Timeline

1715	Treaty of Utrecht
1750	The beginnings of Worcester porcelain with John Wall and William Davis
1777	John Dent founds his famous glove factory
1791	Work starts on the Worcester and Birmingham Canal
1793	Wars against Revolutionary France start
1796	Valentine Green publishes his famous *History and Antiquities of the City and Suburbs of Worcester*
1815	Battle of Waterloo; end of Napoleonic Wars. Worcester and Birmingham Canal opens
1830	Hill, Evans and Co. start producing their Pure Malt Vinegar
1837	Queen Victoria accedes to the throne. Lea and Perrins make up the first jars of their famous sauce
1850	Worcester's first railway station opens at Shrub Hill
1857	Birth of Edward Elgar; he dies in 1934
1883	Birth of Geoffrey Studdert Kennedy (Woodbine Willie); dies in 1929
1899	Boer War between Britain and South Africa commences; lasts until 1902
1900	First performance of Elgar's *Enigma Variations*
1901	Death of Queen Victoria; Edward VII acceeds to the throne. First performance in Worcester of *The Dream of Gerontius*
1906	Royal Commission into the *Existence of Corrupt Practices at the last Election for the City of Worcester*
1914	Outbreak of the First World War; October – Worcesters save the day at the Battle of Gheluvelt
1915	December: Studdert Kennedy joins up, to commence his front-line ministry among the troops
1918	The War ends in November
1929-31	Economic collapse and onset of the Great Depression, affecting all Worcester's industries
1936	Abdication of Edward VIII; accession of George VI
1939	Outbreak of the Second World War; Worcester and the surrounding county prepare to host Royal Family, senior statesmen and government ministries
1940	Worcester is made ready to act as the last line of defence in the event of invasion
1945	Second World War ends
1952	King George VI dies, to be succeeded by Queen Elizabeth II
1964	Basil D'Oliveira joins Worcestershire CCC and plays a major part in the County Championship win the following year
1968	The infamous D'Oliveira Affair prompts South African cricket's international isolation

Bibliography

Atkin, M., *Cromwell's Crowning Mercy: The Battle of Worcester 1651* (Sutton, Stroud, 1998).

Atkin, M., *The Civil War in Worcestershire* (Sutton, Stroud, 1995).

Blair, P.H., *An Introduction to Anglo-Saxon England* (CUP, Cambridge, 1956).

Boden, A., *Thomas Tomkins: The Last Elizabethan* (Ashgate Publishing, Farnham, 2005).

Brierley, M.W., and Byrne, G.A., *Life After Tragedy: Essays on Faith and the First World War* (Cascade Books, Eugene, Oregon, 2017).

Brooks, N., and Cubitt, C., *St Oswald – Life and Influence* (Leicester University Press, London and New York, 1996).

Cannadine, D., 'Orchestrating His Own Life: Sir Edward Elgar as an Historical Personality' in *Elgar: An Anniversary Portrait* ed. Kenyon, N. (Continuum, London, 2007).

Carpenter, J., *Wartime Worcestershire* (Brewin, Studley, 1995).

Church, S., *King John, England, Magna Carta and the Making of a Tyrant* (Macmillan, London, 2015).

Cole, M.H., *The Portable Queen: Elizabeth I and the Politics of Ceremony* (University of Massachusetts Press, USA, 1999).

Craze, M., *King's School, Worcester 1541-1971* (Ebenezer Baylis and Son, Worcester, 1972).

Cunningham, S., *Prince Arthur, The Tudor King Who Never Was* (Amberley Publishing, Stroud, Gloucs, 2016).

Dalwood, H., 'The archaeology of post-Roman and early Medieval Worcestershire' (*West Midlands Regional Research Framework for Archaeology, Seminar 4*).

Dyer, A., *The City of Worcester in the Sixteenth Century* (Leicester University Press, Leicester, 1973).

Evans, E., *Parliamentary Reform 1770-1918* (Longman, London, 2000).

Fay, S., and Kynaston, D., *Arlott, Swanton and the Soul of English Cricket* (Bloomsbury, London, 2018).

Fenwick, J., *St Wulstan of Worcester* (Aldine Press Ltd., Malvern, 1984).

Follet, F.V., *History of the Worcester Royal Grammar School* (Ebenezer Baylis, Worcester, 1950).

Fraser, A., *The Gunpowder Plot* (Weidenfeld and Nicolson, London, 1996).

Frazer, R., *The Mayflower Generation* (Chatto and Windus, London, 2017).

Ed. Goldring, E., Eales, F., Clarke, E., and Archer, J.E. *John Nichols's The Progresses and Public Processions of Queen Elizabeth I* (OUP, Oxford, 2014).

Green, V., *Green's History of Worcester* (London, 1796).

Green, V., *An Account of the Discovery of the Body of King John in the Cathedral Church of Worcester, July 17 1797* (London, 1797).

Grundy, M., *Fiery Glow in Darkness* (Osborn Heritage, London, 1997).

Hanham, H.J., *Elections and Party Management* (The Harvester Press, Sussex, 1959).

http://historywm.com/films/31st-october-1914.

Holmes, R., *Tommy* (Harper Collins, London, 2004).

Hooke, D., *The Anglo-Saxon Landscape: The Kingdom of the Hwicce* (MUP, Manchester, 1985).

Hughes, P. and Leech, A., *The Story of Worcester* (Logaston Press, Herefordshire, 2011).

Hunt, J., *Warriors, Warlords and Saints: The Anglo-Saxon Kingdom of Mercia* (West Midlands History, Alcester, 2016).

Jones, J. R., *Country and Court* (Arnold, London, 1978).

Jones, J. R., *The Revolution of 1688 in England* (Weidenfeld and Nicolson, London, 1972).

Jones, R., *Porcelain in Worcester 1751-1951* (Parkbarn, Worcester, 1993).

Jones, S., 'Voices of War and Peace,' *www.voices of war and peace.org*

Kennedy, M., *Portrait of Elgar* (OUP, London, 1968).

Keogh, B., *The Secret Sauce: A History of Lea and Perrins* (Leaper Books, Worcester, 1997).

Kipling, G., *The Receyt of the Ladie Kateryne* (Early English Text Society, OUP, Oxford, 1996).

Knowles, D., *Bare Ruined Choirs* (CUP, Cambridge, 1976).

Letters and Papers, *Foreign and Domestic, of the Reign of Henry VIII 1509-1547*, 21 volumes in 33 parts, ed. J.S. Brewer, J. Gardiner, R.H. Brodie (London 1862-1910).

Lyes, D. C., *The Leather Glove Industry of Worcester in the Nineteenth Century* (Worcester City Museum and Art Gallery, 1976).

Macaulay, T.B., *The History of England from the Accession of James II*, ed. C. H. Firth (London, 1913-15).

Macdonald, L., *1914* (Michael Joseph, London, 1987).

Mason, E., *St Wulstan of Worcester* (B. Blackwell, Oxford, 1990).

Mylechneest, D., 'A Singular Liberal: Richard Robert Fairbairn and Worcester Politics, 1899-1941,' unpublished M.Phil thesis, University of Coventry, 2007.

Oborne, P., *Basil D'Oliveira: Cricket and Conspiracy, the Untold Story* (Little, Brown, London, 2004).

Oxford Dictionary of National Biography.

Pelling, H., *Social Geography of British Elections, 1885-1910* (Macmillan, London, 1987).

Purcell, W., *Woodbine Willie* (Hodder and Stoughton, London, 1962).

'Report of the Royal Commission to Inquire into the Existence of Corrupt Practices at the last Election for the City of Worcester,' 1906.

Rix, K., 'The Elimination of Corrupt Practices in British Elections: Reassessing the Impact of the 1883 Corrupt Practices Act,' *The English Historical Review*, Vol. CXXIII, Issue 500, 2008, pp. 65-97.

Sandon, J., *Worcester Porcelain* (Shire Library, Oxford, 2009).

Simon, J., *Education and Society in Tudor England* (CUP, Cambridge, 1966).

Spencer, C., *To Catch a King* (William Collins, London, 2017).

Spicer, T., *The Battle of Worcester, 1651* (Paddy Griffith Associates, Withington, 2002).

Townshend, H., *Diary of Henry Townshend of Elmley Lovett 1640-1660* (Worcestershire Historical Society, volumes i and ii, 1915 and 1920).

Vallance, E., *The Glorious Revolution* (Little, Brown, London, 2006).

Walker, I.W., *Mercia and the Making of England* (Sutton Publishing, Stroud, 2000).

Warren, W. L., *King John* (Yale University Press, New Haven, 1997).

Wilks, M., *The Defence of Worcester and the Southern Approaches to Birmingham in World War II* (Logaston Press, Herefordshire, 2007).

William of Malmesbury, *The Life of St Wulstan* (translated by J. H. F. Peile; Llanerch Press, 1996).

Woolwych, A., *Battles of the English Civil War* (B. T. Batsford, London, 1961).

Worcester Cathedral Library and Archive blog.

www.worcestershireregiment.com

www.worcestershiresoldier.org